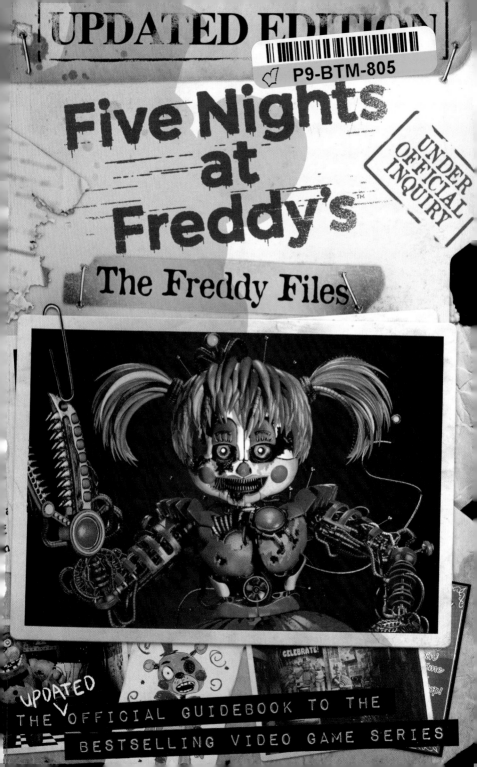

UPDATED EDITION

P9-BTM-805

Five Nights at Freddy's™

The Freddy Files

UNDER OFFICIAL INQUIRY

UPDATED
THE ∨ OFFICIAL GUIDEBOOK TO THE
BESTSELLING VIDEO GAME SERIES

CELEBRATE!

Photo credits: Photos ©: 4 torn paper and throughout: nevermoregraphix/
DeviantArt; 10 graph paper and throughout: rawen713/DeviantArt; 25
bottom: picsfive/Fotolia; 92 bottom left: Marco Govel/Shutterstock;
92 bottom right: Billion Photos/Shutterstock; 144 map: Courtesy Utah
Department of Transportation; 149 wiring diagram: Wire_man/Fotolia; 149
bottom: samiramay/Fotolia; 158 top: Africa Studio/Fotolia; 158 screws:
Andrii Ridnyi/Dreamstime; 159 bottom left: beerlogoff/Fotolia; 159
bottom right: Africa Studio/Fotolia.

ISBN 978-1-338-56381-8

10 9 8 7 6 5 4 3

20 21 22 23

40

Printed in the U.S.A.

First printing 2019

Book design by Off Base and Red Central

Table of Contents

Chapter 1

FIVE NIGHTS AT FREDDY'S

It's the game that launched a million screams.

Five Nights at Freddy's (FNAF) is a point-and-click horror survival game that was founded on a simple enough premise: Last one week working as a night guard in a pizzeria populated by homicidal animatronics. But what evolved from this concept quickly consumed gamers the world over.

Fast forward a bit and (thanks in part to *FNAF*'s startling jump scares) hilarious/terrifying Let's Plays dominated video-sharing sites, fueling the public's curiosity and resulting in billions of views. Still, gamers soon realized there was more to *FNAF* than just deadly animatronics.

Lurking in the darkened corners of Freddy Fazbear's Pizza are the threads of a disturbing mystery. This mystery—hidden throughout the game in posters that change, hallucinations, and even the mysterious fifth animatronic—has kept fans playing and replaying that first game since it was released in August of 2014.

So, what's all the hype about? We're glad you asked.

The Freddy Scoop

The game begins with a "Help Wanted" ad for Freddy Fazbear's Pizza. You'll be working as a security guard on the midnight to 6:00 a.m. shift. The pay is pretty bad at just $120 a week ($4 an hour), but we'll get to that later.

You occupy a stationary position in the office. You can turn to the right or left to see two sets of buttons. One button in each set shuts a door; the other turns on a light outside the door. You can also pull up a monitor to check the security cameras.

HELP WANTED
Freddy Fazbear's Pizza

Family pizzeria looking for security guard to work the nightshift. 12 am to 6 am.

Monitor cameras, ensure safety of equipment and animatronic characters.

Not responsible for injury/dismemberment.

$120 a week. To apply call: 1-555-FAZ-FAZBEAR

Uh, let's see, first there's an
introductory greeting from the company
that I'm supposed to read. Uh, it's kind
of a legal thing, you know. Um, "Welcome
to Freddy Fazbear's Pizza. A magical place
for kids and grown-ups alike, where fantasy
and fun come to life. Fazbear Entertainment
is not responsible for damage to property
or person. Upon discovering that damage or
death has occurred, a missing person report
will be filed within 90 days, or as soon
as property and premises have been thoroughly
... and the carpets have

HEHE

Once you land in the office, the phone starts ringing.

THINGS WE LEARN FROM PHONE GUY

1. Phone Guy apparently worked in the same office, but he's on his last week. If you die (dun dun duuuuuuuun!), "a missing persons report will be filed within ninety days—or as soon as property and premises have been thoroughly cleaned and bleached and the carpets have been replaced." Yep. That sounds like a completely normal thing to say.

2. "If I were forced to sing those same stupid songs for twenty years, and I never got a bath . . ." Why haven't these animatronics been cleaned? Wait—how does one clean an animatronic?

3. The animatronics' servos lock up if they get turned off for too long. The animatronics used to be allowed to walk around during the day, but that was before "The Bite of '87." Apparently someone had a daytime run-in with an animatronic and lost his or her frontal lobe, but survived.

4. Since the animatronics will see you as a metal endoskeleton without its costume on, they'll try to stuff you into a Freddy Fazbear suit. Yikes. So let's avoid that death.

5. You should only close the doors "if absolutely necessary." As Phone Guy says, "Gotta conserve power."

Gameplay and Strategy

You can make five power bars appear by closing both doors, turning on a light, and flipping open the security cameras quickly. But the fifth bar only appears for a second, since you can't have the light on and security cameras open at the same time.

MUTE CALL

12 AM
Night 5

CELEBRATE!

Power left: 91%

Usage:

Without using the doors or lights or checking the cameras, power depletes by about 1 percent every 10 seconds. The in-game clock takes 86 to 90 seconds to pass one "hour," which means you'll lose roughly 9 percent power every hour even if you do nothing.

Using one of your actions—checking the cameras, closing the doors, turning on the lights—adds one bar each to the power indicator, up to four. One action (doesn't matter what it is) drains about 1 percent every 5 seconds, using two actions drains 1 percent every 3 seconds, and using three actions drains 1 percent every 2.5 seconds. To keep this straight, we made you a handy-dandy table.

BWANANANANANANA
MATH MAN!

Number of power bars	Average time it takes to drain 1%	Power drained per hour
1	9.6 seconds	9%
2	4.8 seconds	18%
3	3.2 seconds	27%
4	2.4 seconds	36%

BEWARE OF FOXY.
THE FIRST TIME YOU SLAM THE DOOR ON HIM, HE DRAINS 1 PERCENT POWER; THE SECOND TIME, HE DRAINS 6 PERCENT; THE THIRD TIME, 11 PERCENT AND SO ON, ADDING 5 PERCENT FOR EACH TIME YOU BLOCK.

MAPPING THE ANIMATRONICS AND SPECIAL EVENTS IN FNAF

DINING AREA (1B)
CHICA AND BONNIE APPEAR HERE; FREDDY CAN BE SEEN IN SHADOW.

1A

1B

BACKSTAGE (5)
TERRIFYING DISEMBODIED ANIMATRONIC HEADS.

5

1C

PIRATE COVE (1C)
<u>MOST</u> IMPORTANT CAMERA IN FNAF. KEEP AN EYE ON FOXY.

SUPPLY CLOSET (3)
ONLY BONNIE APPEARS HERE.

3

2A

2B

W. HALL CORNER (2B)
DIRECTLY OUTSIDE OFFICE DOOR.

SHOW STAGE (1A)
FREDDY, BONNIE, AND CHICA START FROM HERE.

= FREDDY

= BONNIE

= CHICA

= FOXY

= GOLDEN FREDDY

7

RESTROOMS (7)
FREDDY AND CHICA PASS THROUGH HERE.

6

KITCHEN (6)
NO VISUALS, BUT THERE IS SOUND.

4A

4B

E. HALL CORNER (4B)
SUPER IMPORTANT FOR LORE!

YOU ARE HERE!

ANIMATRONICS INVENTORY: FREDDY

♦ Appearance: A light brown animatronic bear; wears a black bow tie and black top hat; carries a microphone in his right hand that we're sure he'd find a creative way to kill you with. Enhancing his face shows a handprint across his right eye, and another dark mark (possibly a handprint) along the lower left side of his jaw.

♦ Movements: Show Stage → Dining Area → Restrooms → Kitchen → E. Hall → E. Hall Corner → The Office.

♦ Freddy takes a pretty predictable path, but he's hard to find on the cameras because he stays in the dark most of the time. His glowing silver eyes are the best way to spot him.

♦ In the light, his eyes change color—they're blue when you see Freddy outside the door, but in some jump scares, his eyes are black.

♦ Watching Freddy on the cameras will slow his movements.

♦ Freddy doesn't move until Night 3, unless you run out of power (in which case, he'll get you from the West Hall side of The Office).

IF YOU RUN OUT OF POWER, FREDDY PLAYS THE "TOREADOR SONG" FROM THE OPERA CARMEN.

YOU CAN ALSO HEAR IT PLAYING IN THE KITCHEN WHEN FREDDY'S IN THERE, AND IN THE NIGHT 4 PHONE CALL (ALAS, POOR PHONE GUY).

ANIMATRONICS INVENTORY: BONNIE

♦ Appearance: A bluish-purple animatronic rabbit; wears a red bow tie; plays guitar in the animatronic band.

♦ Movements: Dining Area → Backstage → W. Hall → Supply Closet → W. Hall Corner.

♦ Bonnie is usually the first animatronic to move, and he always sticks to the left (west) side of the restaurant. Bonnie is the only character who appears in the Backstage, Supply Closet, and West Hall Corner. He moves much faster than Freddy or Chica— leading to rumors that he can teleport.

♦ He always enters the office from the west side, and will appear standing in the doorway when the light is turned on.

♦ Of all the animatronics, Bonnie seems to disable the cameras the most as he moves. If he enters the office when the monitor is open, he'll make a raspy groaning noise.

ANIMATRONICS INVENTORY: CHICA

♦ Appearance: A yellow animatronic chicken with an orange beak and magenta eyes; wears a bib that reads "LET'S EAT!"

♦ Movements: Show Stage → Dining Area → Kitchen → Restrooms → E. Hall → E. Hall Corner.

♦ Chica sticks to the right (east) side of the restaurant.

♦ Chica carries an anthropomorphic pink cupcake decorated with two large eyes and teeth. The cupcake disappears when Chica leaves the Show Stage, although a duplicate cupcake can be seen sitting on your desk in the office . . . staring at you creepily . . . the entire game . . .

♦ Chica and Freddy are the only animatronics who enter the Kitchen. You can't see them, but you can hear the clanging of pots and pans.

♦ Chica always enters the office from the East Hall Corner and is visible in the window when the light is turned on.

♦ Like Bonnie, when Chica enters the office, she'll make a raspy groaning noise, cause both the light and door button to become inoperable, and kill the player as soon as they lower the monitor.

. . .OR, SHE'LL JUST PULL DOWN THE MONITOR AND KILL YOU REGARDLESS. BECAUSE APPARENTLY CHICA CAN DO THAT.

CELEBRATE!

Power left: 32%
Usage:

West Hall

ANIMATRONICS INVENTORY: FOXY

♦ Appearance: A reddish-brown animatronic fox with yellow eyes and an elongated snout; wears an eye patch, which is usually flipped up, and has a hook for a right hand. He looks somewhat damaged, with his endoskeleton exposed in a number of places.

♦ Movements: Pirate Cove → W. Hall → W. Hall Corner → The Office.

♦ Foxy always starts at Pirate Cove, behind the curtain. As the night goes on, he starts to peek out more and more until he is entirely revealed. The next time you check the monitor, he's gone. The monitor then flashes to the West Hall camera, where you'll see Foxy sprinting toward the office. He'll attack from the doorway in a matter of seconds unless you close the door in time.

♦ After an unsuccessful attack, Foxy bangs on the door a few times and then returns to Pirate Cove to begin the cycle again. Unfortunately, every time that he is blocked by the door, he drains the player's power: 1 percent the first time, then an additional 5 percent every time thereafter. (See notes on power consumption.)

KEEPING FOXY AT BAY MEANS CHECKING ON HIM JUST ENOUGH, BUT NOT TOO OFTEN.

Codes, Glitches, and Secrets

So, just be aware, the cha[...]
to wander a bit. Uh, they'[...]
kind of free roaming mode [...]
Something about their serv[...]
they get turned off for to[...]
used to be allowed to wal[...]
the d[...]

HOLD DOWN C, D, AND + TO SKIP A NIGHT.

y parts
[...]ght of
d teeth
[...]ite human [...]ask,
e,

CLICK ON THE POSTER IN THE OFFICE TO HONK FREDDY'S NOSE.

3 AM
Night 1

Show Stage

Power left: 60[...]
Usage[...]

TRY CHANGING YOUR COMPUTER'S DATE TO HALLOWEEN, OCTOBER 31, AND BOOTING UP THE GAME.

[...]
tr[...]
a [...]
wo[...]
weren[...]
animatronic devi[...]
facial area. So,
having your head forcefull[...]

GOING ON A BEAR HUNT

In the West Hall Corner (camera 2B) is a poster of Freddy, which has a very small chance of changing. The poster becomes a close-up of Freddy's face, but his fur is golden, and there aren't any eyes in the mask. Once the poster changes, drop the monitor and an empty animatronic suit, "Golden Freddy," will appear in the office, alongside flashes of IT'S ME. Seeing him will cause the game to crash, but you can avoid this by bringing up the monitor again quickly.

SEE PAGE 24

You can also trigger Golden Freddy by inputting 1/9/8/7 on the custom night. You won't see the scene of the empty animatronic suit in the office, though.

RARE SCREENS

After you've plowed through all five nights at Freddy's, beaten the sixth night, and tried your hand at the custom night, don't miss these rare screens! Some of these play a huge role in popular fan theories.

SHOW STAGE (1A): This secret screen can only be found in the game files, but we think it's worth a peek nonetheless.

PIRATE COVE (1C): After Foxy has left Pirate Cove, the stage sign changes to IT'S ME. See page 24.

W. HALL CORNER (2B): Check this camera and you may see the poster change to an image of Freddy ripping his head apart.

E. HALL (4A): Posters are replaced with images of crying children.

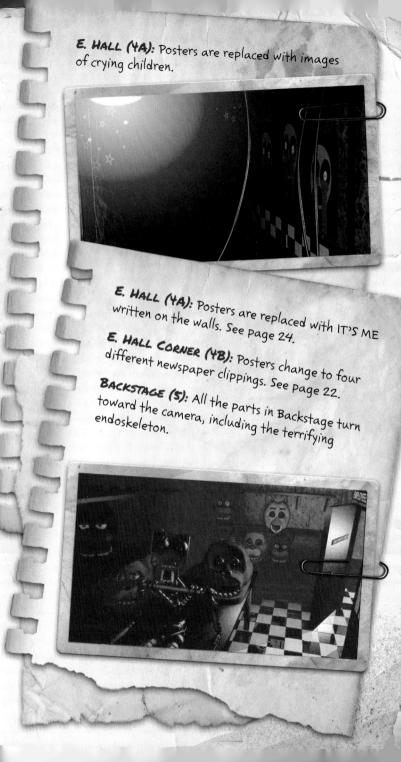

E. HALL (4A): Posters are replaced with IT'S ME written on the walls. See page 24.

E. HALL CORNER (4B): Posters change to four different newspaper clippings. See page 22.

BACKSTAGE (5): All the parts in Backstage turn toward the camera, including the terrifying endoskeleton.

Lore and Theories

FAN THEORIES: THE BITE OF '87

Phone Guy mentioned "The Bite of '87," in which someone was attacked by an animatronic and lost his or her frontal lobe. This event is why the animatronics' movements are restricted during the day. A lot of theories have popped up around which character was responsible.

♦ **FOXY.** The most obvious answer. After all, there is an out of order sign on Pirate's Cove. Plus Foxy seems to have the sharpest teeth, and some have insisted that his jaw appears to be dislocated.

12 AM
Night 5

E. Hall Corner

GOLDEN FREDDY. A less likely contender is Golden Freddy. He has the same handprint marks on his face as regular Freddy. Similar to Foxy, he appears to be out of order—just a mascot suit without its endoskeleton. AND when you input 1/9/8/7 as the levels of the animatronics on the custom night, who should appear but Golden Freddy? Seems suspicious.

FREDDY. The Rules for Safety in the E. Hall Corner say "Don't touch Freddy," but they don't mention other animatronics. Freddy also appears to have handprints on his face . . . Was someone fighting him off? Theorists have pointed out that the handprints match the placement of Freddy's hands on the poster of him ripping apart his head. However, while the position of his hands does match with the handprints, Freddy only has four fingers, and the handprint has five.

RULES FOR SAFETY

1. Don't run.
2. Don't yell.
3. Don't scream.
4. Don't poop on floor.
5. Stay close to mom.
6. Don't touch Freddy.
7. Don't hit.
8. Leave before dark.

thank you,
management

Fan Theories: The Missing Children

If you really want to dig into the story of the game, keep an eye on the E. Hall Corner, where the Rules for Safety will change to a series of newspaper clippings that reveal the horrific secret lurking at the heart of the game:

- ♦ Kids Vanish at Local Pizzeria—Bodies Not Found
- ♦ Five Children Now Reported Missing. Suspect Convicted.
- ♦ Local Pizzeria Threatened With Shutdown Over Sanitation.
- ♦ Local Pizzeria Said To Close By Year's End.

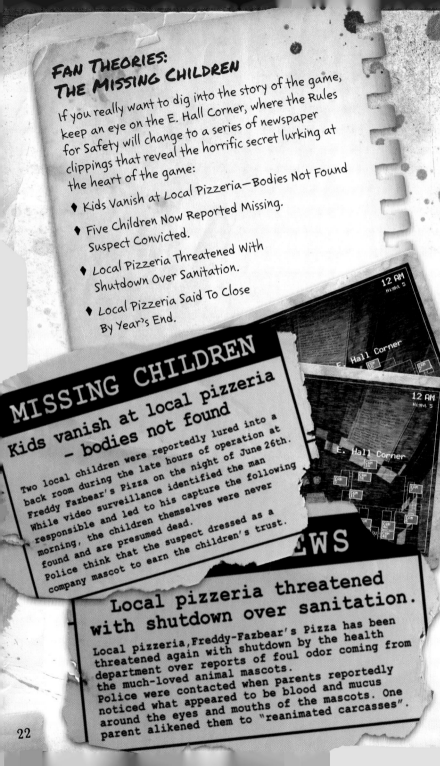

MISSING CHILDREN
Kids vanish at local pizzeria – bodies not found

Two local children were reportedly lured into a back room during the late hours of operation at Freddy Fazbear's Pizza on the night of June 26th. While video surveillance identified the man responsible and led to his capture the following morning, the children themselves were never found and are presumed dead. Police think that the suspect dressed as a company mascot to earn the children's trust.

Local pizzeria threatened with shutdown over sanitation.

Local pizzeria, Freddy-Fazbear's Pizza has been threatened again with shutdown by the health department over reports of foul odor coming from the much-loved animal mascots. Police were contacted when parents reportedly noticed what appeared to be blood and mucus around the eyes and mouths of the mascots. One parent alikened them to "reanimated carcasses".

Local pizzeria said to close by year's end.

After a long struggle to stay in business after the tragedy that took place there many years ago, Freddy Fazbear's Pizza has announced that it will close by year's end.
Despite a year-long search for a buyer, companies seem unwilling to be associated with the company.
"These characters will live on. In the hearts of kids- these characters will live on." - CEO

Power left: 69%
Usage:

Five children were apparently lured to a back room by someone who wore a mascot costume to gain the kids' trust. A suspect was arrested and charged, but the bodies of the children were never found and they were presumed dead. Shortly thereafter, customers complained of odors and reported seeing blood and mucus around the eyes and mouths of the animatronics, implying that the bodies of the children were stuffed inside Freddy and his friends. This matches Phone Guy's words from Night 1—if you were to be stuffed inside a suit, "the only parts of you that would likely see the light of day again would be your eyeballs and teeth, when they pop out the front of the mask."

One thing seems certain—the animatronics themselves have been possessed by the spirits of the dead children, looking for revenge.

ll Corner

MISSING CHILDREN

Five children now reported missing. Suspect convicted.

Five children are now linked to the incident at Freddy Fazbear's Pizza, where a man dressed as a cartoon mascot lured them into a back room. While the suspect has been charged, the bodies themselves were never found.
Freddy Fazbear's Pizza has been fighting an uphill battle ever since to convince families to return to the pizzeria. "It's a tragedy."

Fan Theories: "It's Me"

This phrase recurs in hallucinations throughout the game: on the Pirate's Cove sign, the East Hall walls, with Golden Freddy's appearance, and in-game flashes as early as Night 1. When you receive your paycheck, you'll learn that your name is Mike Schmidt.

Several theories have popped up connecting this phrase to Mike:

♦ The souls of the children are taunting Mike.

♦ Mike has a connection to the children—maybe he's a parent or sibling posing as a security guard to gain access to the pizzeria in order to learn more about the cover-up. The kids are trying to get through to Mike that it's them possessing the animatronics.

♦ Mike *is* the killer, or was otherwise complicit in the deaths of the kids. He is hallucinating this phrase because his guilty mind is shouting out that *he's the murderer*. Maybe a little far-fetched, but it would answer why the animatronics are so desperate to kill Mike. Phone Guy's endoskeleton explanation of the animatronics' motives doesn't seem to line up with the events of the game—after all, Bonnie routinely enters the Backstage, sees the costume-less endoskeleton sitting on the table, and never tries to stuff it into a costume.

Fazbear's "Twisted" Pizza Recipe*

Ingredients:

Two 1 lb. loaves frozen bread (roll) dough
Pizza sauce
Shredded mozzarella cheese
Mini pepperonis
Parmesan cheese
Italian seasoning
Flour

Thaw the bread dough and roll it onto flour-covered boards. Shape into half-inch thick rectangles. Spread the pizza sauce lightly on one rectangle, then sprinkle with the mozzarella cheese and pepperonis. Place the second dough rectangle on top of the first one and press it together before slicing into one-inch wide strips. Twist these strips and sprinkle with Parmesan cheese and Italian seasoning (if desired) before placing them onto a baking sheet. Bake at 400 degrees for fifteen to twenty minutes, or until the sticks are golden brown. Use extra pizza sauce for dipping.

* KIDS, ASK A PARENT TO HELP YOU!

Chapter 2

FIVE NIGHTS
AT FREDDY'S 2

The terror continues in *Five Nights at Freddy's 2* (*FNAF2*), a game which pushed many players to the limit in terms of . . . multitasking? Yes, there is a *lot* here to manage, and that's putting it mildly. Eleven animatronics roam the floor, looking to kill you or crash your game if you stare at them long enough—not to mention the other four animatronics that are apparently just there to populate your nightmares. Plus there's a frighteningly long list of to-dos: Keep the music box wound, keep the vents clear, strobe that flashlight in Foxy's direction . . . More animatronics now have a set of unique instructions (similar to Foxy from *FNAF*), so there are plenty of details to juggle.

Also new to *FNAF2* are the "death mini-games" that are triggered with jump scares. Each mini-game has a creepiness factor off the charts and has spawned a flurry of theories about the rapidly expanding mystery at the heart of Freddy Fazbear's Pizza.

The game is also chock-full of new revelations from Phone Guy, like the two *additional* Freddy's locations, one of which he calls "Fredbear's Family Diner," the seeming origins of the franchise. But we're getting ahead of ourselves. Let's start with Night 1.

The Freddy Scoop

We Meet Again . . . Phone Guy

Sounds like Phone Guy is still alive, so this game likely takes place before the events of the last one. That, or Phone Guy is immortal. Once again, you're working as a security guard on the midnight to 6:00 a.m. shift for Freddy Fazbear's Pizza, but the layout of the place is completely different. . . and there are no doors. Because why would a security office need doors?

Uh, hello? Hello, hello? Uh, hello and welcome to your new summer job at the new and improved Freddy Fazbear's Pizza. Uh, I'm here to talk you through some of the things you can expect to see during your first week here and to help you get started down this new and exciting career path.

Uh, now, I want you to forget anything you may have heard about the old location, you know. Uh, some people still have a somewhat negative impression of the company. Uh... that old restaurant was kind of left to rot for quite a while, but I want to reassure you, Fazbear Entertainment is committed to family fun and above all, safety. **LIES!** They've spent a small fortune on these new animatronics, uh, facial recognition, advanced mobility, they even let them

28

HELP WANTED

Grand Re-Opening!!!

Vintage pizzeria
given new life!

Come be a part of the
new face of Freddy
Fazbear's Pizza!

What could go wrong?

$100.50 a week!
To apply call:
1-555-FAZ-FAZBEAR

HERE'S WHAT PHONE GUY REVEALS:

1. Something very bad happened at the "old location," so Fazbear Entertainment spent a lot of money on their new animatronics, including facial recognition systems that interface with criminal databases.

2. The animatronics weren't programmed with a proper "night mode," so they wander around looking for people. As a temporary solution, a music box has been placed in the Prize Corner. Its music should keep one of the animatronics at bay.

3. You've been supplied with an empty Freddy Fazbear head to wear as a mask. When you wear it, any animatronic that comes into the office will see you, think you're one of them, and wander back out again.

4. This Freddy head won't work on Foxy, unfortunately, but shining your flashlight on him should make him go away.

5. The building lights will never run out of power, but the flashlight will.

6. Old animatronics are sitting creepily in the back room, but they're now used for spare parts. (These *look like* the animatronics from *FNAF*, but they're not exactly the same. Check the animatronics inventory for specifics.)

As we've come to expect from *FNAF*, things tend to unravel quickly. On Night 4, we learn the restaurant is being investigated and may need to close temporarily, as someone seems to have tampered with the animatronics' facial recognition systems. On Night 5, the restaurant is put on lockdown, with no one allowed in or out—especially prior employees.

END-OF-NIGHT HALLUCINATIONS

When you first boot up the game, as well as at the end of Nights 2, 3, and 4, you'll experience a nightmare. In it, you're wearing the Freddy Fazbear head and can only see a peek of what looks like the empty dining area from *FNAF*.

The first time, you'll see Bonnie and Chica on either side of you and hear unseen children laughing. The game will then crash, and code saying "err" will appear in the upper left corner of the screen. Night 2 features a repeat of this nightmare, but now Bonnie and Chica are looking at you. On Night 3, Bonnie and Chica appear angrier than before, and Golden Freddy stands right in front of you. The fourth and final time, Golden Freddy has disappeared, but Bonnie and Chica remain. The Puppet blocks your view no matter which way you look.

When the game crashes on Nights 2 through 4, a different code appears in the upper left corner of the screen: "it's me."

Hello? Hello... uh... what on earth are you doing there, uh didn't you get the memo, uh, the place is closed down, uh, at least for a while. Someone used one of the suits. We had a spare in the back, a yellow one, someone used it... now none of them are acting right. Listen j-just finish your shift it's safer than ~~ in the midd~~

make
f
when
pr
good n

NIGHT 6

After completing Night 5, Jeremy Fitzgerald (you) receives a paycheck for $100.50. This amount probably would have felt more significant in 1987. In any case, making it this far brings up a menu option for a sixth night. Phone Guy will tell you that the restaurant is being closed down after one final event scheduled for tomorrow—a birthday party.

Your reward for making it through an extra night? An overtime paycheck for a measly $20.10.

ROBOTS SCRAP
Freddy Fazbear's is C

After
a f
Freddy
is close

The n
will be
possibl
howev
char
kept in super
ossible reorganization
of the company.

"It's a minor setback.
We are confident that
we will reopen someday
budget." - CEO Fazbear Ent

even if it is with a much small

PAY TO THE: Jeremy Fitzgerald
Twenty dollars and 10/100

Overtime

DATE 11-12-1987   142

$ 20.10

DOLLARS @

Fazbear Entertainment

THE END

142
DATE 11-12-1987
PAY TO THE: Jeremy Fitzgerald $ 100.50
ORDER OF
One hundred dollars and 50/100   DOLLARS @

MEMO Welcome to the family   Fazbear Entertainment

THE END

CUSTOM NIGHT

As in the first game, surviving the first six nights unlocks a custom night which allows you to change the AI settings of each animatronic. New this time around is a series of ten pre-set difficulties. For nine of them, beating the night unlocks a collectible toy for the office desk; beating the 10/20 mode, or "Golden Freddy" challenge, earns you a star.

```
Five
Nights
at
Freddy's
2
★ ★

New Game
>>Continue
         Night 5
6th Night
Custom Night

v 1.03                Press and hold delete to reset all data.
```

```
Customize Night

Freddy   Bonnie   Chica    Foxy      BB
< 20 >   < 20 >   < 20 >   < 20 >    < 20 >

Toy      Toy      Toy      Mangle    Golden
Freddy   Bonnie   Chica              Freddy
< 20 >   < 20 >   < 20 >   < 20 >    < 20 >

(0-2)easy (3-6)med (7-12)hard (13-20)extreme

<          Golden Freddy          >      READY
```

So, aside from some desk swag, what reward do you get for surviving a custom night? Nothing more than a termination notice, made out to—who the heck is Fritz Smith? Looks like Jeremy *did* get switched over to the day shift after Night 6.

Interestingly, they fire Fritz for the same reasons they fire Mike from *FNAF*: "Odor" and "Tampering with animatronics."

GREAT!!
(Now get out.)

PINK SLIP

You're fired.

Reasons: ...ith animatronics

THE END

Character AI Settings

Game Mode	Freddy	Bonnie	Chica	Foxy	BB	Toy Freddy	Toy Bonnie	Toy Chica	Mangle	Golden Freddy
20/20/20/20	20	20	20	20	0	0	0	0	0	0
New & Shiny	0	0	0	0	10	10	10	10	10	0
Double Trouble	0	20	0	5	0	0	20	0	0	0
Night of Misfits	0	0	0	0	20	0	0	0	20	0
Foxy Foxy	0	0	0	20	0	0	0	0	20	10
Ladies Night	0	0	20	0	0	0	0	20	20	0
Freddy's Circus	20	0	0	0	10	20	0	0	0	0
Cupcake Challenge	5	5	5	5	5	5	5	5	5	5
Fazbear Fever	10	10	10	10	10	10	10	10	10	10
Golden Freddy	20	20	20	20	20	20	20	20	20	20

< 5 > < 5 > < 5 > < 5 >

(0-2)easy   (3-6)med   (7-12)hard   (13-20)extreme

Golden Freddy < 5 >

★ < Cupcake Challenge > ★ READY

Gameplay and Strategy

ANIMATRONICS INVENTORY: BALLOON BOY

- Appearance: At last, a *human* animatronic that wants to kill you! Balloon Boy wears a red-and-blue striped shirt and a propeller beanie. He carries a balloon as well as a sign that reads—what else?—"BALLOONS!"

- Movements: Game Area (10) → Left Vent (5) → The Office.

- Once he starts moving, you won't see him anywhere else, but you'll hear him! He calls out "Hello?" and "Hi!" and sometimes giggles.

- The fourth time that you hear him calling out, expect to catch sight of Balloon Boy in the Left Vent. Don the Freddy head immediately to get rid of him.

- Although Balloon Boy doesn't kill you, he might as well. If he gets into the office, he'll disable the flashlight and vent lights, leaving you completely helpless.

ANIMATRONICS INVENTORY: THE PUPPET
(AKA THE MARIONETTE)

♦ Appearance: The Puppet is a lanky black creature with white stripes on his arms and legs and a white face with painted cheeks and lips.

♦ Movements: The Puppet is inside the large gift box in the Prize Corner (11). If the music runs out and you jump to the Prize Corner fast enough, you can still wind the music box so long as he still appears in the camera shot. If he's gone, you're toast.

♦ When the music runs out, and the Puppet leaves the Prize Corner, you can catch a quick glimpse of him in the Main Hall before he kills you.

♦ Unfortunately, there is no way to stop the Puppet's attack, so keep the music box playing.

Freddy's Fun Fact

The music box song, "My Grandfather's Clock," was written in 1876 by Henry Clay Work. The tune was so well-known that a "longcase" clock became known as a "grandfather clock." The song is about a clock that worked for ninety years, responding to a man's joys and sorrows, until it rang an alarm on his deathbed and stopped working entirely when he died.

ANIMATRONICS INVENTORY: TOY CHICA

♦ Appearance: This Chica is made of glossy plastic; her bib reads "LET'S PARTY!"

♦ Movements: Show Stage (9) → Main Hall (7) → Party Room (1) → Left Vent → The Office. Toy Chica will also appear in Party Room (4) and the Office Hallway (she won't attack from here). She is less active on later nights.

♦ After leaving the Show Stage, her eyes and bill are missing.

ANIMATRONICS INVENTORY: WITHERED CHICA

♦ Appearance: This Chica is worn down, but noticeably different from *FNAF* Chica; note the less-rounded frame, all-yellow legs, and three toes.

♦ Movements: Parts/Service Room (8) → Party Room (4) → Party Room (2) → Right Vent (6) → The Office.

♦ Withered Chica can *not* be seen using the flashlight in the Right Vent's blind spot. She'll move directly from the Right Vent (6) to the office.

ANIMATRONICS INVENTORY: TOY BONNIE

♦ Appearance: A glossy plastic Bonnie with green eyes and buck teeth.

♦ Movements: Show Stage → Party Room (3) → Party Room (4) → Party Room (2) → Right Vent (6) → The Office.

♦ Toy Bonnie is usually one of the first animatronics to move, but he is less active on later nights.

ANIMATRONICS INVENTORY: WITHERED BONNIE

♦ Appearance: Still a giant blue rabbit, but Withered Bonnie is missing his face.

♦ Movements: Parts/Service Room (8) → Main Hall (7) → Party Room (1) → Left Vent (5) → The Office. Withered Bonnie can also enter the Office from the Office Hallway.

♦ Withered Bonnie can *not* be seen by turning on the light in the Left Vent blind spot.

♦ Very active starting Night 3.

ANIMATRONICS INVENTORY: TOY FREDDY

- ♦ Appearance: Glossy plastic version of Freddy; has two buttons on his belly.
- ♦ Movements: Show Stage (9) → Game Area (10) → Office Hallway → The Office.
- ♦ Toy Freddy isn't very active, and is even less active on later nights. But if he does make it to the Office, wearing the Freddy head will keep him from entering.

ANIMATRONICS INVENTORY: WITHERED FREDDY

- ♦ Appearance: Slightly different from *FNAF* Freddy; now has two buttons on his belly.
- ♦ Movements: Parts/Service Room (8) → Main Hall (7) → Party Room (3) → Office Hallway → The Office.
- ♦ Starts moving on Night 2; more active on Night 3.

ANIMATRONICS INVENTORY: MANGLE

♦ Appearance: Proof that toddlers can destroy almost anything. With white and pink features and a visible endoskeleton, Mangle doesn't look like Foxy at all.

♦ Movements: Kid's Cove (12) → Prize Corner (11) → Game Area (10) → Main Hall (7) → Party Rooms (1 or 2) → Right Vent (6) → The Office. Mangle can appear in the Office Hallway, but it won't enter from here.

♦ When Mangle is in the Right Vent; don the Freddy head. You'll hear static as it approaches. If it gets in the Office, it'll stay until ending your game.

♦ Mangle is extremely active! It leaves Kid's Cove right at midnight on Night 2.

ANIMATRONICS INVENTORY: WITHERED FOXY

♦ Appearance: This Foxy is more tattered than in *FNAF*. He has one animatronic ear completely exposed and several tears showing his endoskeleton.

♦ Movements: Parts/Service Room (8) → Office Hallway → The Office.

♦ Scare Foxy off with the flashlight. The Freddy head has no effect on him.

MAPPING PATHS OF THE TOY ANIMATRONICS

PRIZE CORNER (11)
THE MOST IMPORTANT CAMERA; WIND THE MUSIC BOX FROM HERE.

KID COVE (12)
"THE MANGLE" LIES HERE... BUT NOT FOR LONG!

RIGHT VENT (6)
TOY BONNIE AND MANGLE ENTER THE OFFICE FROM HERE.

PARTY ROOMS (1-4)
ANIMATRONICS APPEAR HERE ON THEIR WAY TO VENTS IN 1 AND 2.

THE OFFICE
TOY FREDDY WILL APPROACH AND ATTACK FROM THE OFFICE HALLWAY.

LEFT VENT (5)
TOY CHICA AND BALLOON BOY ENTER THE OFFICE FROM HERE.

= TOY FREDDY
= TOY BONNIE
= TOY CHICA
= MANGLE
= BALLOON BOY

OFFICE

41

Codes, Glitches, and Secrets

SECRET ANIMATRONICS

GOLDEN FREDDY

Unlike *FNAF*, nothing specific triggers Golden Freddy. He is active on Night 6 and in the custom night—randomly appearing in the Office Hallway as a ghostly head, or in the Office itself as a crumpled animatronic suit. Quickly equip the Freddy mask to prevent Golden Freddy's attack.

ALMOST EVERYTHING ABOUT THIS GAME IS DIFFERENT, BUT ONE THING STAYED THE SAME: CLICK ON THE POSTER IN THE OFFICE TO HONK FREDDY'S NOSE.

RWQFSFASXC AND SHADOW FREDDY

A shadow version of Freddy occasionally appears in the Parts/Service Room. An animatronic known as RWQFSFASXC, or Shadow Bonnie, can occasionally be seen standing on the left side of the office. Looking at RWQFSFASXC for too long will cause your game to crash.

ENDOSKELETON

A bare endoskeleton can be seen in the Prize Corner and Left Vent, though it never attacks the player. There are some interesting fan theories about which animatronic this endoskeleton belongs to.

BALLOON GIRL?

An animatronic like Balloon Boy (but with pink eyes) is sometimes staring at you from under your desk. This animatronic never appears elsewhere in the game and cannot kill you.

FNAF·2 RETRO ARCADE

Death Mini-game: SAVETHEM

Dying in *FNAF2* might trigger one of several mini-games rendered in 8-bit graphics. These are perhaps the most talked-about element of the game because they're so different from anything we've seen before. The first mini-game is known as SAVETHEM (the phrase spelled by the letters you will hear being called out). Using the keyboard for movement (W=up, A=left, S=down, D=right), you, as Freddy, follow the Puppet through a map of the restaurant until reaching the Prize Corner. You'll pass slumped-over children and pools of blood along the way.

On rare occasions, "Purple Guy" will end the mini-game early. If Purple Guy appears, a scrap of code will appear in the lower left corner following the game crash: "you can't."

Death Mini-game:
Take Cake to the Children

This post-death mini-game has Freddy taking cake to six children (with another child visible outside the room). Walking into the kids changes their color to green—if you turn them all green at once, you lose control of Freddy. Neglecting the kids changes their color to red. Midway through the game, a car pulls up outside. The aforementioned Purple Guy exits and kills the crying child, who turns gray. The letters being called out are "S-A-V-E-H-I-M"... but you can't. In fact, you move slower and slower until all of the children turn red. The mini-game ends with a jump scare courtesy of the Puppet.

It's important to note that Freddy looks slightly different in this mini-game than he does in SAVETHEM. The mini-game map here is also the smallest. These discrepancies have an important bearing on some fan theories.

45

FNAF·2 RETRO ARCADE

Death Mini-game: Foxy Go! Go! Go!

Here you'll play as Foxy. Leaving the previous room, you enter a room full of children as party poppers go off. When the last one goes off, you're returned to the starting position and must make your way to the kids once again. And then again. But the last time you do, Purple Guy is visible in the lower left corner of the room. He's smiling. In the next room, the children are dead. This post-death mini-game ends with a Foxy jump scare.

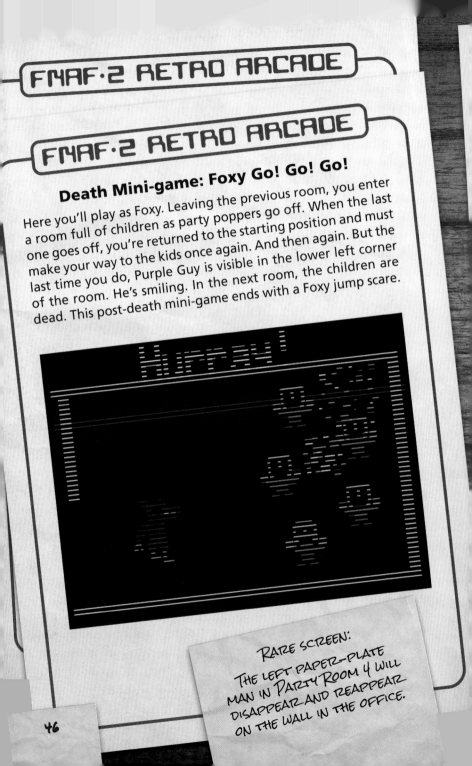

RARE SCREEN:
THE LEFT PAPER-PLATE MAN IN PARTY ROOM 4 WILL DISAPPEAR AND REAPPEAR ON THE WALL IN THE OFFICE.

Death Mini-game: Give Gifts, Give Life

In this post-death mini-game, you play as the Puppet. Per the on-screen instructions, you need to give gifts to four apparently dead children. Returning to the center of the room, you're told to "Give Life." As you approach each child, the head of an animatronic appears over the child's head. Once again, letters are being called out: "H-E-L-P-T-H-E-M." You're also earning a score for giving the gifts, but the numbers change to a random sequence when the mini-game ends with Golden Freddy's jump scare.

Slowing down the playback of the mini-game just before the jump scare reveals a fifth child in the center of the room. Golden Freddy's jump scare originates from the child; perhaps implying that the Puppet placed a fifth animatronic head (Golden Freddy's) on this child.

Lore and Theories

FAN THEORIES: SEQUEL VS. PREQUEL AND ALTERNATE FREDDY'S LOCATIONS

It's now widely accepted in the *FNAF* community that *FNAF2* takes place before *FNAF*. The evidence?

1. Phone Guy dies in *FNAF*, but he's alive in *FNAF2*.

2. Still-Alive-Phone Guy reveals that the animatronics walk around during the day; but in *FNAF* their movements are restricted to nighttime because of The Bite of '87.

3. The newspaper clipping at the end of *FNAF2*, Night 6 says that the new (read: toy) animatronics are being "scrapped due to possible malfunctions" but that the original characters "are being kept in hopes of a possible reorganization of the company."

4. The newspaper clipping also reveals that the owners are looking to create a smaller-scale version of the restaurant. Notice how much smaller the *FNAF* restaurant is compared to *FNAF2*.

But that's not all. Phone Guy reveals another interesting tidbit about the timeline—TWO additional Freddy's locations. He tells us on Night 1 that a previous location was left to rot after something terrible happened there, and then later, on Night 5, we learn there was an original restaurant called "Fredbear's Family Diner" which was apparently franchised out to create the other locations.

Fan Theories: The Bite of '87.

Is it a coincidence that *FNAF2* is set in 1987 and yet we hear nothing about The Bite of '87? Many theorists are convinced the bite *did* happen during the game, even if we didn't realize it.

What We Know about the Bite

It happened in 1987, during the day, and the victim lost a large segment of his or her brain, but survived. The victim's age is never mentioned. After the bite, the animatronics were only allowed to move around at night.

Theory: The Bite Happened on Day 4 to the Day Guard

On Night 4, Phone Guy tells you to avoid eye contact with the animatronics, as they've "been acting very unusual, almost aggressive towards the staff," yet the animatronics have been acting normal with the kids. Thus, the animatronics would not have attacked the children, but they *would* have attacked a guard. On Night 5, Phone Guy tells you that a day-shift "position just became . . . available," possibly implying that the day guard was injured by an animatronic earlier that day.

Theory: The Bite Happened at the Birthday Party . . . and You're the Victim

Still others believe that the bite happened after Night 6, at the birthday party that Phone Guy mentions in his last message. The evidence? Theorists believe that the available day shift position mentioned on Night 4 is because Purple Guy—the killer—was the day guard. Thus, when Phone Guy tells you to report to the birthday party, wear your uniform, and stay *very* close to the animatronics, you're in the perfect position to get bitten.

Fan Theories: The Mini-Games Reveal Multiple Killings

A prominent strain of theory maintains that each of the four mini-games in *FNAF2* reveals a different set of murders.

SAVETHEM is believed to be the *FNAF2* restaurant—the mini-game map is similar to the camera map. There are five dead children here as well. Purple Guy also looks different; he's now wearing something gold on his chest and holding something in his hand.

FOXY GO! GO! GO! has a completely different map which now has two rooms (Pirate's Cove and a Party Room). The game reveals that five children are murdered.

TAKE CAKE TO THE CHILDREN is believed to take place at Fredbear's Family Diner, since the map consists of only one room/a street (denoting a smaller location) and the playable Freddy looks different from the Freddy in SAVETHEM (meaning an older version of Freddy). Theorists assert the game shows Purple Guy's first murder.

Take cake to the chil

GIVE GIFTS, GIVE LIFE shows five dead children as well as the Puppet, but at a seemingly different location (it's one room, but the room's dimensions are different from Take Cake).

ON A FINAL, DISTURBING NOTE, THE MODELS FOR DEAD CHILDREN ARE DIFFERENT FROM GAME TO GAME, SUPPORTING THEORISTS' CLAIMS THAT THERE COULD BE FOUR UNIQUE SETS OF VICTIMS.

Fan Theories: What We Know about the Killer

♦ He's associated with the color purple. Duh. The real question is, what does the purple coloring mean? This could be part of his uniform, or something else.

♦ He might be a security guard. In SAVETHEM, Purple Guy has a golden object pinned to his chest. This has led many to believe that he's a security guard, and the object is a badge.

♦ He may know how to work the animatronics. In Night 4, you're instructed not to make eye contact with the animatronics, as "someone may have tampered with their facial recognition systems." All signs point to Purple Guy as the culprit. After all, if he's in the criminal database, he would need to disable their facial recognition to sneak into Freddy's.

♦ He was likely an employee of Freddy's. Phone Guy on Night 5 warns: "The building is on lockdown, uh, no one is allowed in or out, you know, especially concerning any . . . previous employees." Though it's never explicitly stated, why would Phone Guy give this warning if the wrongdoing wasn't committed by an employee?

♦ He uses a "yellow suit" to kill. On Night 6, Phone Guy tells you that "Someone used one of the suits. We had a spare in the back, a yellow one, someone used it . . . now none of them are acting right." This matches what we know from the newspaper clippings in *FNAF*: "A man dressed as a cartoon mascot lured (the children) into a back room."

♦ So who is he? There are a few theories circulating. Aside from the theory that Purple Guy is just a random security guard at Freddy's operating the day shift, Phone Guy is a suspect for many. People say that the rare Purple Guy kill in SAVETHEM shows Purple Guy holding a phone—a clear link between the two. Others believe Purple Guy could be you—in those end-of-night hallucinations, you're clearly *inside* a mascot costume, just like the killer. Plus maybe those hallucinations of "it's me" are the confessions of a guilty mind: "It's me, I did it. I killed those kids." Yeesh. Talk about a tell-tale heart.

Chapter 3

FIVE NIGHTS AT FREDDY'S 3

If you thought it was impossible for *FNAF* to take a darker turn, allow us to introduce you to *Five Nights at Freddy's 3* (*FNAF3*). Set thirty years after the horrific events that took place at Freddy Fazbear's Pizza (though which *specific* events we're not sure), this game operates on two disturbing levels.

In the present, you're working at a horror attraction built around the mythos of the infamous murders. Only one animatronic is real, but the "phantoms" (read: hallucinations) of other animatronics also appear every now and again to mess with you. A perpetually failing network of ventilation, audio, and cameras adds to the torment, and needs constant attention.

In a series of seven mini-games, you're working to gain closure for the souls of the five children who were murdered at the hands of Purple Guy many years ago. The mini-games are difficult to access, must be completed in the correct order, and, even after you do successfully complete them, your current night gets reset. It can be a frustrating process, but one that's ultimately satisfying.

The Freddy Scoop

It's the dawn of a new era for *FNAF*, and—since Old Phone Guy is most likely dead—that means a new Phone Guy. New Phone Guy explains that it's been thirty years since the last Freddy Fazbear's Pizza shut down, and a company is trying to capitalize on the restaurant's gruesome past by launching "Fazbear's Fright: The Horror Attraction." The attraction opens next week, so they have to make sure everything works and NOTHING CATCHES ON FIRE. (Always important.) After talking to the original designer of the building, the company finds a boarded-up room inside the restaurant that they're planning to investigate. On Night 2, New Phone Guy reveals they've obtained a real animatronic—Springtrap—which they're using for the attraction. It's loose inside the building, but don't worry . . . it'll find you.

COMING SOON!

Fazbear's Fright: The Horror Attraction!

Local amusement park is getting ready to scare your socks off with a new attraction based on the unsolved mysteries of Freddy Fazbear's Pizza.

Featuring actual relics from the decades-old pizzeria, this new attraction is guaranteed to bring back your childhood in the worst possible way.

THINGS WE LEARN FROM OLD PHONE GUY'S TRAINING CASSETTES

In addition to the Springtrap animatronic, New Phone Guy also found some old training tapes, recorded by—you guessed it—Old Phone Guy!

SPRING LOCK SUITS

♦ At one point, Freddy's had two "spring lock" suits that doubled as animatronics and mascot costumes.

♦ To wear the suits as a costume, you use a handcrank to "recoil and compress the animatronic parts around the sides of the suit." Spring locks must be fastened tight in order to keep the animatronic parts compressed, leaving room for a human occupant. The slightest pressure or moisture can cause the spring locks to trip, releasing the machinery and crushing the person inside the suit.

♦ When the spring lock suits are in animatronic mode, they're pre-set to walk toward any sound they hear.

♦ On Night 4, Old Phone Guy informs you of an incident at the restaurant's "Sister Location" involving multiple spring lock failures, at which point the company deemed the suits unsafe and retired them.

Hey-Hey! Glad you came back for another night! I promise it'll be a lot more interesting this time. We found some—some great new relics over the weekend. And we're out tracking down a new lead, right now. So—uh lemme just update real quick, then you can get to work. Like, the attraction opens in like, a week, so we had to make sure everything works, and nothing catches on fire! Uh—when the place opens, people will come in at the opposite end of the building, and work their way towards you, then past you and out the exit. Uh—yeah. You've officially become a part of the attraction. Uh—You'll be starring as ... The security guard! So only will you be monitoring the cameras as they

Also gleaned from Old Phone Guy's audio is the existence of "safe rooms" within each restaurant.

SAFE ROOMS

♦ There is a designated "safe room" in every Freddy's location. This room is not included in the digital map programmed into the animatronics, or in the building's security blueprints. This room is "hidden to customers, invisible to animatronics, and is always off camera," meaning there are no security cameras in these rooms.

♦ On Night 4, Phone Guy reminds employees, "Under no circumstance should a customer ever be taken into this room and away from the show area."

♦ On Night 6, it's announced that the room is being sealed, and that employees should never talk to anyone else of its existence. No one is allowed to enter the room to collect their belongings, either.

NIGHT END MINI-GAMES

At the end of each night, a mini-game begins with you in control of an animatronic (Freddy, Bonnie, Chica, Foxy). The goal is to follow Shadow Freddy through the restaurant toward the safe room. After you try to enter the safe room, expect to be dismembered by Purple Guy . . . ending the mini-game and the night.

Although you will always need to "die" to continue to the next night, you are still able to wander a short distance. Heading to the left is the Parts/Service Room; among the parts, there appears to be a human skull. If you continue down past the "Pirate Cove" area into a hallway, you'll find hints for unlocking the mini-games required to access the "good" ending.

SEE PAGES 68-75 FOR MINI-GAME HINTS.

follow me.

follow me.

follow me.

follow me.

NIGHT 5 END MINI-GAME

On Night 5, you control a crying child during the post-night mini-game. Go toward the safe room as before, and you'll see dismembered animatronics along the way. You're now able to enter the safe room where the animatronics could not go before. Once inside, you'll notice four crying children blocking Purple Guy from leaving the room. Eventually, he dons what appears to be the empty spring lock suit; sure enough, it soon malfunctions and crushes him.

REVENGE!

If you play the game straight through, after the Night 5 end mini-game, you'll see an image of broken animatronic heads, each with a lit eye. Faded text in the background reads "Bad ending."

NIGHTMARE MODE!

As with the two prior games, a more difficult night is unlocked after the fifth, called simply (and most appropriately) "Nightmare." On this night, the ventilation system fails a lot more quickly than it normally does, so get ready for a challenge!

NIGHTMARE

If you beat the game's Nightmare mode, regardless of how you played the mini-games, you'll see a newspaper informing you that the attraction has burned to the ground due to faulty wiring. But . . . is that Springtrap watching from the background in the article's picture? Maybe this isn't the end of the Freddy's saga after all.

IT BURNS!

Fazbear's Fright burns to the ground!

A new local attraction based on an ancient pizzeria chain burned down overnight.

Authorities have not ruled out foul play, but at the moment it seems to have been caused by faulty wiring.

Very little was found at the scene. The few items that were salvaged will be sold at public auction.

THE BLURRED TEXT AROUND THE ARTICLE CONTAINS DEVELOPMENT STORIES FROM GAME CREATOR SCOTT CAWTHON.

Gameplay and Strategy

REVENGE OF THE MATH

Not counting failure due to a phantom animatronic, you have a certain number of audio uses before the system goes down. Your number of uses changes each night.

	Night 1	Night 2	Night 3	Night 4	Night 5
Audio Uses	unlimited	10	4	3	2

The camera system will go down more rarely than the other systems. This mainly results from overuse. The ventilation system most frequently fails due to phantom animatronics. Similar to the audio, the other two systems fail more frequently as the week progresses.

Note that it takes about five seconds each to restart the cameras, audio, or ventilation. It takes about nine seconds to reboot them all at once. If two or more systems go down, we recommend rebooting everything.

Animatronics Inventory: Springtrap

(AKA "Spring Bonnie"?)

- Appearance: A tarnished yellow spring lock animatronic rabbit.

- Movement: Springtrap is *FNAP*'s first free-roaming animatronic—he has no set starting position and can move through every single room and the vents.

- Springtrap is the only real animatronic in this game, and the only one that can kill you!

- When Springtrap approaches the office, he'll slink past the window. If you see him there, you'd better think fast.

- Use the audio device to lure Springtrap to adjacent rooms, but it won't work if he's more than one room away.

- Springtrap likes to use the vents—if he enters a room with an adjoining vent, it's best to seal it off just in case. Double-click on a camera to seal the connecting vent.

- Springtrap only moves to rooms adjacent to his last position or connected to it by an air vent. Don't lose sight of him—he's very hard to find.

Trapping Springtrap:

It's best to bounce Springtrap between cameras 9 and 10. If he gets closer, use the audio to get Springtrap into the camera 5 room, then close off the vent. You can trap him in there for a while using the audio and keeping the vents closed.

63

PHANTOM INVENTORY:

In addition to Springtrap, there are loads of animatronic hallucinations to deal with. All of them will cause systems to malfunction unless you take quick action, and suspiciously, all the animatronics appear burned.

PHANTOM FOXY

Phantom Foxy randomly appears in the office. Quickly pull up the cameras or maintenance panel to avoid his jump scare.

DISABLES CAMERA

PHANTOM FREDDY

Appears in the hallway (seen through the window) moving right to left before appearing inside the office. Avoid a jump scare by watching the cameras or maintenance panel until he passes.

PHANTOM MANGLE

Phantom Mangle appears on camera 4, hanging from the ceiling and screeching. It will then appear in the office behind the window unless you lower the monitor or switch cameras as soon as Mangle appears.

PHANTOM PUPPET

The Phantom Puppet appears on camera 8. Switch to another camera fast or it will appear in the office and block you from using the maintenance panel and monitor.

DISABLES AUDIO

DISABLES VENTILATION

PHANTOM BALLOON BOY

Can appear in any camera except vents.

PHANTOM CHICA

Randomly appears in the arcade machine monitor on camera 7.

65

Mapping the Animatronics and Special Events in FNAF3

Camera 8
Double-click Balloon Boy poster for BB's Air-Adventure mini-game.

Phantom Puppet also appears here.

Camera 7
Use arcade machine to access Mangle's Quest mini-game.

This is also where Phantom Chica appears.

Camera 6
Note the cupcake for Chica's Party mini-game.

11

7

12

8

6

13

1

REMEMBER, SPRINGTRAP CAN APPEAR ANYWHERE ON THE MAP AND HAS NO SET PATH.

9

10

14

5

4

2

3

15

OFFICE

CAMERA 4
PHANTOM MANGLE APPEARS HERE. NOTE THE CUPCAKE FOR CHICA'S PARTY MINI-GAME.

CAMERA 3
NOTE THE CUPCAKE FOR CHICA'S PARTY MINI-GAME.

CLICK THE PUPPET POSTER FOR HAPPIEST DAY MINI-GAME.

THE OFFICE
TILES ON THE WALL OPEN STAGE 01 MINI-GAME; BONNIE TOY ON THE DESK OPENS SHADOW BONNIE'S MINI-GAME.

CAMERA 2
NOTE THE CUPCAKE FOR CHICA'S PARTY MINI-GAME.

Path to the Good Ending

In order to view the game's "good" ending, players must complete a number of mini-games in a specific order. Hints to these mini-games appeared throughout the night-end mini-games in the walls of a room one left and three down from the Show Stage room.

FNAF·3 RETRO ARCADE

Mini-game: BB's Air Adventure

The night-end mini-game hint for BB's Air Adventure was: "BBdblclick"—a word jumble. Double-clicking on the Balloon Boy poster visible on camera 8 brings up this mini-game.

Controlling Balloon Boy with the keyboard (A=left, D=right, W=jump), your task is to collect all of the balloons. **Do not** go through the exit door when it appears, however. Instead, jump onto the platform above the exit and then jump toward the left wall.

It's actually possible to pass through this barrier—doing so will send you to a pixelated gray screen with some terrifying dead Balloon Boys. Move to the right and you'll find a new playfield containing an additional, rainbow-colored balloon. Jump through the left wall to reenter the mini-game and collect the final balloon. This will restart your night in the main game.

FNAF·3 RETRO ARCADE

Mini-game: Mangle's Quest

This game is only accessible on Night 2! The night-end mini-game hint for Mangle's Quest was a series of squares that corresponds to button presses. Look for the arcade machine on camera 7, and click on the machine's buttons in the following order: top left, bottom left, top right, bottom right.

In this mini-game, collect all of Mangle's parts without running into a child. If successful, an exit door should appear. **Do not** leave through that door. Instead, find the secret opening in the wall above the door and jump through it. You'll enter a new screen, this time pixelated and red, with a large, crying version of what looks like the Puppet. Move to the left, and you'll enter a new section of the mini-game where you'll need to jump onto each balloon platform. Follow the path and a cake will appear on the final platform. Collect it to reset your night.

Mini-game: BB's Air Adventure

Reenter the game, same as before. Just like the first time, jump through the secret opening above the exit after collecting the balloons. This time, however, you'll land on a series of balloon platforms. Jumping carefully from one to the next, you'll wind up on a blue platform with a crying gray child. Since you collected the cake in Mangle's Quest, you can now give it to the child to cheer him up . . . and end the mini-game. Your night will reset.

Mini-game: Chica's Party

The night-end mini-game hint for Chica's Party appeared as four cupcakes. This mini-game must be accessed on Night 3; to unlock it, you must click on four cupcakes located throughout the attraction. They can be found on the floor of the camera 2, 3, and 4 rooms, and atop the arcade machine in the camera 6 room. Look for a small skull with black eyes.

As Chica, jump and grab all the cupcakes you can find and deliver them by walking up to the children in the next room. There's also a hole in the floor that leads to two additional children and two additional cupcakes to deliver.

However, to get the good ending, jump down through the hole in the floor and enter the next screen. Standing on the platform at the top left, jump to the left two more times to enter into a secret screen. On this screen you'll see two more balloon platforms that lead to another dead child. Walk up to the child to serve them another huge cake. Doing so will exit the mini-game and reset the night.

FNAF·3 RETRO ARCADE

Mini-game: "Stage 01"

This mini-game can only be accessed on Night 4. The night-end mini-game hint for Stage 01 appeared as a numerical code: 395248. The code corresponds to wall tiles in the office, left of the desk, arranged in a 3x3 grid. Click on each tile as you would dial a phone: top right (3), bottom right (9), dead center (5), top center (2), center left (4), and bottom center (8).

In this mini-game, players control Golden Freddy entertaining children with Springtrap. Jump toward the children to "glitch" through the wall on the left side of the room. As you fall, you'll see that same stage room, twice, until you hit the ground. There are actually nine playing fields arranged in a 3x3 grid. All of them are the same except for the top right (3) and middle right (6)— room six, oddly, only has two children. Follow the path in the map below to get to room three and deliver cake to a lone crying child.

FNAF·3 RETRO ARCADE

Mini-game: Shadow Bonnie

The hint for this night-end mini-game appeared as a shadow version of Bonnie. To access the final mini-game, look for a shadowy figurine of Bonnie on the right side of the office desk on Night 5. Double-click on it.

This mini-game is a mash-up of the ones seen previously, but you're given a new power—pressing "S" phases the character from one game setting into a new purple room, and pressing "S" again phases the character into the other mini-games you've played.

There's a child at the bottom left corner of the purple room, but outside the walls. To reach it, press "S" to cycle through the various mini-games until you land inside BB's Air Adventure. Remember the glitch that allowed you to pass through the left wall? Jump to the upper left platform and into the wall, passing through it and falling to the ground. Walk to the center of the screen and press "S" to phase back to the purple room. You are now outside the walls and can approach the child to give it cake.

FNAF·3 RETRO ARCADE

Mini-game: Happiest Day

This mini-game can be accessed on any night. To find it, bring up the monitors and switch to camera 3. Look for two posters on the right side of the room. Double-click on the left poster, closest to the center of the room, to start the mini-game.

As the Puppet, walk past all the partygoers with their cakes. In the last room is a gray crying child being watched over by other gray children wearing masks of the animatronics. When you give the child a cake, it stops crying and is given a mask of its own (Golden Freddy). All the masks fall to the ground as the children disappear. Meanwhile, balloons rise into the air, and the mini-game ends.

THE GOOD ENDING

If you beat the game after going through the mini-games properly, you'll see the same ending image as before, except now there are no lights in the animatronics' eyes. Curiously, the fifth animatronic head (which most believe belongs to Golden Freddy) is missing from the line-up. Faded text in the background reads "the end."

YOU CAN HONK FREDDY'S NOSE IN FNAF3 BY CLICKING ON THE POSTER IN THE

Codes, Glitches, and Secrets

EXTRAS OPTION

There is no "custom night" in *FNAF3*. However, beating Night 5 opens up an Extras option in the main menu. From here, players can view the animatronics' jump scares, play the mini-games (as long as the "good" ending was unlocked), and enable some fun cheats. You can speed up time, equip a Springtrap "radar" (to help you find him more easily), and even increase Springtrap's aggression level. (We'll pass on that last one.)

RARE SPRINGTRAP IMAGES

There are three rare Springtrap images that can appear randomly before the menu screen. All three show that there is someone *inside* the Springtrap suit. Someone long dead.

CAMERA 2

Retro Freddy poster changes to Spring Bonnie.

CAMERA 4

The Bonnie poster will change to a pink cupcake or a golden cupcake.

The Office

Crumpled Freddy suit sometimes appears in the corner of the office.

The Office

Two paper plate characters appear on the walls of the office.

Camera 10

Retro Freddy poster changes to Spring Bonnie.

Lore and Theories

FAN THEORIES: SHADOW BONNIE/SHADOW FREDDY

Though introduced in *FNAF2*, Shadow Bonnie and Shadow Freddy don't really take center stage until *FNAF3*. Shadow Freddy plays a crucial role in the night-end mini-games, while Shadow Bonnie has his own role to play in the good-ending mini-games. Just who are these characters, and what are their intentions?

One theory maintains that Shadow Freddy and Shadow Bonnie are the ghosts of the Freddy's employees who were killed by the spring lock suits. On Night 4, Phone Guy mentions "*multiple, simultaneous spring lock failures*" at Freddy's sister location. Some fans maintain that "multiple" simply means that several spring locks within one suit failed, but what if he meant that two suits killed two employees at the same time?

Theorists believe this explains why the shadow animatronics want to help the dead children—as the ghosts of employees, they feel guilt at not being able to stop the murders.

- Both animatronics appear in *FNAF2*, meaning that they likely died prior to the events of *FNAF2*.

- They don't seem to have a physical form. Shadow Freddy is able to enter the safe room in *FNAF3*, and goes unnoticed by Purple Guy. None of the other animatronics can enter because the room is not programmed into their internal map. In the mini-games, Shadow Bonnie's figure seems to dissipate and re-form often. He is also able to travel to different mini-games, something none of the other mini-game animatronics can do.

- They help the children. In the night-end mini-games, Shadow Freddy tries to lead you to the killer, who's hiding out in the safe room. In his mini-game, Shadow Bonnie gives cake to one of the children.

- They could be linked to the killer. Note the purple coloring of the shadow animatronics and the purple color associated with the killer.

follow me.

Fan Theories: Golden Freddy Was a Spring Lock Suit

There's been a lot of speculation about Golden Freddy—where he came from, why he seemingly can't move, and why he appears and disappears randomly. One theory says that *FNAF3* provides us with the answer: Golden Freddy is a spring lock suit.

Theorists point to the crumpled sitting position of Golden Freddy, and how it matches the sitting position of the empty Springtrap suit in the night-end mini-game on Night 5. Fans also believe this could answer why Golden Freddy appears and disappears like a hallucination—the spring lock suits were retired (and presumably destroyed) long ago. All that would remain is a ghost of the animatronic.

Still, others reject this idea on the basis that Golden Freddy has four-fingered hands, which would be awkward for a human occupant. Springtrap has five fingers.

Chica's Golden Cupcake Pizzas*

Ingredients:
1 can (8 oz) triangle dinner rolls
Pizza sauce
Mini pepperonis
Shredded mozzarella cheese
Italian sausage, pre-cooked

Spray a cupcake pan with cooking spray. Separate the eight triangle dinner rolls and press each one into a cup. In a separate bowl, mix about a half cup of pizza sauce with mini pepperonis, shredded mozzarella cheese, and pre-cooked Italian sausage. Spoon the mixture into each cup, then top with additional mozzarella cheese. Bake at 350 degrees for 16 to 18 minutes or until the edges are lightly browned.

* KIDS, ASK A PARENT TO HELP YOU!

8

Chapter 4

FIVE NIGHTS AT FREDDY'S 4

Five Nights at Freddy's 4 (FNAF4) marks a huge next step for the series. Gone are the security office, the stationary playable character, and the . . . well, the paycheck wasn't worth much to begin with. But for all this change, FNAF4 kept the elements players like best: 8-bit mini-games at the end of each night, perhaps the most nightmare-inducing animatronics of any game to date, and mysterious Easter eggs that have become the hallmark of the series.

That said, this game is *punishing*. It forces you to crank up the volume in order to hear a variety of subtly distinct sounds. Failing to respond correctly to those sounds results in an eardrum-shattering jump scare that will likely send you (and possibly your keyboard) flying.

Beyond the gameplay, there's a lot to be gleaned here in terms of lore, and FNAF4 kicked off one of the most intense fan-theory debates in the series' history—The Bite of '87 vs. The Bite of '83—as well as the million simultaneous cries of "What's in the box?"

Let's dig into some of these questions and more.

The Freddy Scoop

FNAF4 begins with a screen that announces "5 days until the party" followed by an 8-bit image of a little yellow Freddy wearing a purple hat. His name is Fredbear, and he reveals that you've been locked in your room.

The screen dissolves, and you'll see yourself as a crying (but alive) child in a bedroom with plush toys. The aforementioned Fredbear is a stuffed animal on your bed whose creepy eyes follow your every movement . . .

Using the keyboard (W=up, A=left, S=down, D=right), make your way toward the (locked) bedroom door. You won't be able to open it, but that's okay. The screen dissolves—tomorrow is another day.

5 days until the party.

After the mini-game, you'll find yourself launched into the primary gameplay. You're playing as a child, trying to ward off nightmare versions of the animatronics who are attacking you in your bedroom.

Like the other games, you need to survive from midnight until 6:00 a.m. by checking your closet, the hallways outside your room, and your bed, where the nightmare animatronics lurk. Before each night begins, you'll also have the chance to skip two hours by playing a mini-game with a plush version of Springtrap.

YOUR ALARM CLOCK WILL FLASH A RANDOM SERIES OF NUMBERS AT THE END OF EACH NIGHT BEFORE HITTING 6:00 A.M.

Though the primary gameplay will take up the majority of your time, there are a number of 8-bit-type mini-games at the end of each night. The games unravel a story.

FNAF·4 RETRO ARCADE

Night 1 End Mini-game

Four days until the party. You are the crying child once again, but this time, the bedroom door is unlocked. Fredbear tells you that someone is hiding, and he won't stop until you find him. Exit your room to find a hallway with a grandfather clock. To the right is a peachy-pink bedroom. Heading back and to the left, you'll end up in a living room with a TV. Walk into the TV to be jump-scared by your older brother and end the mini-game.

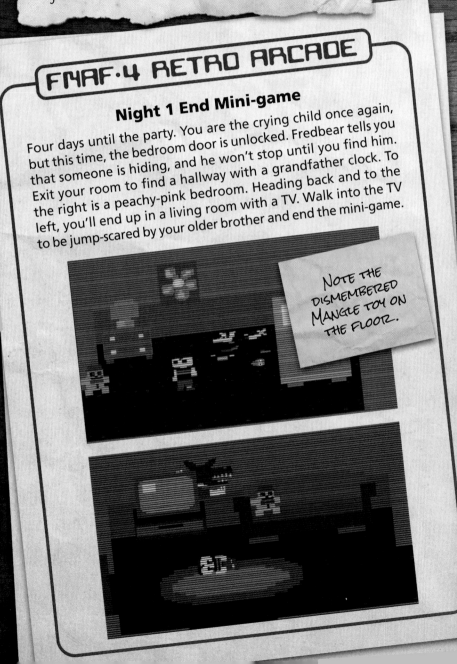

Note the dismembered Mangle toy on the floor.

Night 2 End Mini-game

Three days until the party. Tonight you're at a Freddy's restaurant, but which incarnation we're not sure. Someone has left without you—someone who knows you hate this place. The game urges you to run toward the exit. If you go left, the game prompts you with "No! Don't you remember what you saw?" A man in a Fredbear suit then arrives, blocking the exit to your right. The game tells you to "Find someone who will help! You know what will happen if he catches you!"

On the next screen, you're urged to run past a silhouetted Freddy and Spring Bonnie, but walking forward ends the mini-game.

Night 3 End Mini-game

Two days until the party. You're back at the pizzeria, but this time you can escape. On the way home, talk to the various kids you see—one child reveals that the upcoming party is your own birthday party. From the restaurant door, head down and follow the sidewalk left and then up to get home. From here, head to the right and down into your bedroom to be jump-scared and end the mini-game.

Night 4 End Mini-game

One day until the party. Judging by the endoskeletons and the Fredbear suit, it appears you're locked in the spare parts/ maintenance room of the pizzeria. Unable to escape, you once again end up crying on the floor, begging to be let out, until the mini-game ends.

Night 5 End Mini-game

Zero days until the party. Tonight you're back at the pizzeria with no control—you just have to watch this time. Your brother and his friends (all wearing animatronic masks) tease you until they force you up at eye level with the Fredbear animatronic. Your head ends up in Fredbear's mouth, followed by a sickening crunch as the animatronic bites down.

Night 6 End Mini-game

Once again, you can only sit and watch the ending of the story. As the kid sits in the spotlight with the plush Fredbear, you hear someone tell you they're sorry. Then someone tells you that you're broken, but that the speaker will put you back together. As Fredbear and the child fade away, you can hear the sound of a heart monitor flatlining.

You're broken.

NIGHT 7

Beating Night 7 brings up a screen with an image of a locked box. You can click on the locks to rattle them, but they won't open. The text reads, "Perhaps some things are best left forgotten, for now."

Gameplay and Strategy

SOUNDS

Like we said, this game is punishing on sound—you need to learn how to tune your ear to hear *everything*. Here's a list of what to listen for.

SOUNDS YOU SHOULD DISREGARD:

♦ Dog barking

♦ Clock chimes
(Good luck. Those chimes are *loud*.)

♦ Distorted radio

Sounds to listen for:

- Breathing: Before you turn on your flashlight at the doorway, be sure to listen for breathing as it means an animatronic is outside your room. If you hear it, shut the door and don't open it until you hear . . .

- Footsteps on gravel: This means an animatronic is walking away from or toward your room.

- Deep, slow-motion laugh: Nightmare Fredbear/Nightmare has entered your room.

- Metallic-sounding giggles: Freddles are accumulating on the bed behind you.

- Dishes clanking: Chica is in the kitchen . . . for now.

- Pitter-patter running, followed by a creak: Nightmare Foxy has entered your closet.

Sound is oriented to where you are in the room, so if you hear a sound from your left, you should check the left door. This includes when you're at the door and can hear breathing, laughing, or other sounds.

And of course, listen carefully for the sweetest sound of all:

The alarm clock hitting 6:00 a.m.

Hours are exactly sixty seconds long, making each night last exactly six minutes.

= NIGHTMARE FREDDY

= NIGHTMARE BONNIE

= NIGHTMARE CHICA

= NIGHTMARE FOXY

RIGHT HALLWAY DOOR
Nightmare Chica only enters from this side.

YOU ARE HERE!

CLOSET
Nightmare Foxy hides here if he enters your room.

LEFT HALLWAY DOOR
Nightmare Bonnie only enters from this side.

BED
Nightmare Freddy only approaches from the bed.
Be sure to clear the Freddles!

NIGHTMARE FREDBEAR AND NIGHTMARE CAN APPEAR ANYWHERE!!!

ANIMATRONICS INVENTORY: NIGHTMARE FREDDY

- Appearance: He's still the brown bear we've come to know and fear, just a lot more tattered and torn than ever before, and with a monstrous jaw to boot. There are also three miniature animatronics, called "Freddles," attached to his body.

- Movements: Nightmare Freddy will attack if you do not check the bed often enough. Freddles will appear on the bed, but flee when you shine the flashlight on them.

- The more Freddles on the bed, the longer it takes to clear them.

IF YOUR FLASHLIGHT FLICKERS, IT MEANS YOUR FREDDLE COUNT IS INCREASING

ANIMATRONICS INVENTORY: NIGHTMARE BONNIE

- Appearance: Bonnie is still a large, bluish-purple rabbit, but some of his features, such as his teeth and claws, appear to be exaggerated. His red bow tie is just about the only part of him not in tatters.

- Movements: Nightmare Bonnie appears in the left hallway and can attack from there or the center of the bedroom. He will only attack in the bedroom if you haven't checked the left hallway in a while.

- Nightmare Bonnie is very active on the first few nights.

SOMETHING INTERESTING TO NOTE— THE FULL-SIZE ANIMATRONICS IN *FNAF4* HAVE FIVE FINGERS, WHEREAS MOST OF THE PREVIOUS GAMES' ANIMATRONICS (EXCEPT SPRINGTRAP) HAVE FOUR.

NIGHTMARE BONNIE
AND NIGHTMARE
CHICA STICK TO THE
SAME SIDES OF THE
MAP AS THEIR *FNAF*
COUNTERPARTS.

ANIMATRONICS INVENTORY:
NIGHTMARE CHICA

♦ Appearance: If you thought her yellow feathers and orange beak made her sort of cute before, think again! Nightmare Chica appears shredded from head to toe, and has mismatched eyes alongside monstrous claws and teeth.

♦ Movements: Nightmare Chica appears in the right hallway and can attack players there. While she does not enter the bedroom like Bonnie, her cupcake does, and it's just as scary and dangerous as Chica herself.

♦ Nightmare Chica is very active on the first few nights.

ANIMATRONICS INVENTORY:
NIGHTMARE FOXY

♦ Appearance: Nightmare Foxy is similarly a much larger, more tattered version of the familiar fox. He's got a sharp hook for a right hand, but is lacking the pirate eye patch.

♦ Nightmare Foxy doesn't appear until Night 2. You'll hear his fast footsteps in either hallway followed by a creak as he enters the closet. You'll also see the closet door open/close slightly when he enters.

♦ Movements: As he did in Pirate Cove way back in *FNAF*, Nightmare Foxy goes through a sequence before attacking from the closet. First, he'll appear in the closet as a plush. Next he appears standing upright, his head not visible. After that, you'll see him in a crouching position with his jaw visible. Finally, his head pokes out of the closet, and he may snap at you with a mini-jump scare.

♦ To placate Nightmare Foxy, hold the closet doors closed until he regresses to an earlier pose.

ANIMATRONICS INVENTORY: NIGHTMARE FREDBEAR

- Appearance: A giant, terrifying version of the Fredbear we've been seeing in the mini-games. This tattered and torn bear animatronic has golden fur and wears a purple hat and bow tie.

- Movements: He can attack from either hallway, the closet, or the bed . . . basically from everywhere!

- Nightmare Fredbear only shows up on Night 5 and Night 6 (after 4:00 a.m.). When he's around, however, none of the others will be.

- Audio clues will help you determine where Nightmare Fredbear is coming from. If you hear laughter, he'll appear on the bed or in the closet. If you hear laughter followed by footsteps, he's in the hallway.

ANIMATRONICS INVENTORY: NIGHTMARE

- Appearance: A giant, terrifying version of the Fredbear we've been seeing in the mini-games, but completely black with a yellow hat and bow tie.

- Movements: As with Nightmare Fredbear, Nightmare appears from both hallways (but closer), in the closet, and on the bed.

- Nightmare only appears on Night 7 and Night 8 after 4:00 a.m.

- Nightmare gives the same audio clues as Nightmare Fredbear.

NIGHTMARE IS MUCH
HARDER TO SEE
AT A GLANCE, SINCE
HE BLENDS IN WITH
THE SHADOWS.

MINI-GAME: FUN WITH PLUSHTRAP

Between nights, you can play a mini-game called Fun with Plushtrap to remove two hours from the clock (game starts at 2:00 a.m. instead of midnight).

Your goal is to get Plushtrap to land on an X marked on the floor. The kicker is that neither Plushtrap nor the X are visible unless you turn on your flashlight. When you flick the flashlight on, Plushtrap will either go limp where he stands or hide in an adjacent room. If you don't check on him enough, Plushtrap will jump-scare you; check on him too often and he won't make it to the X within the time limit.

To win, listen closely and wait for the sound of footsteps. Plushtrap will get up from the chair and start walking forward.

Turn on your flashlight each time you hear a few seconds of running to judge where he is.

102

Codes, Glitches, and Secrets

EXTRAS MENU

Beating Night 5 unlocks the Extras menu, allowing players to view animatronics, a "Making of . . ." gallery progression, jump scares, mini-games, Nightmare mode, and cheats. Some of these options remain locked until players complete Night 6.

Cheats include a map of the house with a "radar" of the animatronics, faster nights (thirty seconds instead of sixty seconds each), and a danger indicator near the hallway doors.

NIGHT 8

Though there is no "Custom Mode" in *FNAF4*, there is still a way to play 20/20/20/20. Enter the new Extras menu and type "20202020" to access this final challenge. All the animatronics are set to their maximum difficulty level, and Nightmare does appear after 4:00 a.m.

NIGHT-END MINI-GAME EASTER EGGS

Night 2: When you're urged to run past a silhouetted Freddy and Spring Bonnie, turn back to the right first to get a glimpse of Purple Guy helping someone into the Spring Bonnie suit. This is our only glimpse of Purple Guy in *FNAF4*.

Night 3: The girl with pigtails along your walk home reveals that the animatronics "come to life at night" and that "if you die, they hide your body and never tell anyone." On the previous screen, a kid holds a Spring Bonnie plush.

> You'd better watch out! I hear they come to life at night.

Night 3: Click on the TV in the living room to watch the *Fredbear & Friends* TV show. Notice the copyright date: 1983.

TRY CLICKING THE NOSE OF THE PLUSH FREDDY ON THE BED.

RARE SCREENS

Don't miss these rare screens in *FNAF4*, which point to a darker plot twist. Turning around to clear Freddles from the bed, you may get one of these three rare screens, which show a pill bottle, an IV, and a vase of flowers on your bedside table.

HALLOWEEN EDITION

The *FNAF4* Halloween update replaces Nightmare with Nightmarionne, Nightmare Bonnie, and Nightmare Chica with jack-o'-lantern versions of each, and Nightmare Foxy with Nightmare Mangle. The Fun with Plushtrap mini-game becomes Fun with Balloon Boy.

The update also alters the night-end mini-games to fit the Halloween theme (check out the Halloween decor in the house and at Freddy's).

Explore the Extras menu for terrifying new challenges including Blind Mode, Mad Freddy, Insta-Foxy, and All Nightmare.

Lore and Theories

FAN THEORIES: THE BITE OF '83 VS. THE BITE OF '87

In *FNAF4*, did we witness the infamous Bite of '87? Or was it another bite entirely?

TEAM '83

♦ *Fredbear & Friends*: In the Night 3 mini-game, the TV plays a show with a 1983 copyright date.

♦ Responsibility: If this is The Bite of '87, why are the animatronics blamed for the kids tossing a child into Fredbear's mouth? And, since the animatronic was stationary on the stage, why restrict the animatronics' movement?

♦ Frontal Lobe: The Bite of '87 victim lost his or her frontal lobe. When you remove the frontal lobe from the brain, it no longer feels fear. This seems inconsistent with our apparent gameplay as the bitten child.

Team '87

- **Teasers:** The *FNAF4* teaser campaign featured animatronics with text asking, "Was it me?" Theorists believe this points toward The Bite of '87, since the animatronic that committed the bite is hotly contested within the fandom.

- **Mangle:** A Mangle toy can be seen on the floor of the girl's bedroom on Nights 2 and 3. Since some theorists believe that Phone Guy recorded the *FNAF2* tapes in 1987, and we're told on those tapes that Mangle is a new addition to Freddy's, theorists insist this puts the game squarely in 1987.

- **Plush Freddy:** The plush Freddy on the bed seemingly has a twin at the Prize Corner in *FNAF2*, which many theorists believe takes place in 1987.

- **Radio Static:** Occasionally you'll hear radio static during gameplay. It's actually a backward recording of the *FNAF* Night 1 phone call, in which Phone Guy mentions The Bite of '87.

Fan Theories:
What's up with Fredbear?

It probably escaped no one's notice that your Fredbear plush follows you around a lot in the night-end mini-games. He's present in every screen outside of the restaurant, even though you don't appear to be carrying him from room to room. Also, his silver eyes follow you as you move. Almost like . . . a camera.

Some theorists believe that the main character of *FNAF4* is being spied on, for reasons we don't seem to know. But at the end of the game, your Fredbear plush does give you a scrap of an answer:

> "You're broken . . . I'm still here.
> I will put you back together."

Could whoever is spying on you be able to put your soul into an animatronic?

I will put you back together.

Fan Theories:
The Kids Who Look Like Animatronics

According to theorists, there are three kids here who look oddly like animatronics we've seen in other *FNAF* games. Could these kids have been the inspiration for the three animatronics, or is it just an Easter egg that has no bearing on canon?

Balloon Boy

The Puppet

Baby

Chapter 5

FIVE NIGHTS AT FREDDY'S: SISTER LOCATION

If you thought *FNAF4* was a departure, allow us to introduce you to *Five Nights at Freddy's: Sister Location*, the game that took the series in a completely different direction. For the first time in *FNAF*, you're out of the one-room setup and allowed (mostly) free rein of the building. Added to your night-guard duties are various maintenance tasks, including repairing the animatronics, which you somehow have to do *without* getting murdered by them.

The series continues to get darker with the introduction of Ennard (try explaining this character to your grandma) as well as a number of mysterious Easter eggs that have launched a whole new string of theories. This game also features a full cast of voice characters in the animatronics, who are—not surprisingly—pretty talkative. With the added dialogue comes some quirky humor, a refreshing light in this deep and winding saga.

But perhaps the biggest change for the series is the absence of, well, Freddy's. *Sister Location* is set at Circus Baby's Pizza World—an apparent warehouse of animatronics. The animatronics live here, but they're rented out for parties.

There's a lot to unpack, so let's get started.

The Freddy Scoop

As you boot up the game, you'll overhear a conversation between an unnamed man and "Mr. Afton." Afton apparently designed the animatronics you'll meet in this game. The unnamed man notes some questionable design choices in the robots, but you never hear the end of the conversation.

Similar flashback audio will play at the start of the following nights, but this time you'll hear a little girl—Mr. Afton's daughter—talking. She begs her father to play with Circus Baby, at one point asking, "Didn't you make her just for me?"

At the end of Night 5, you'll hear an ominous line implying the girl may have been killed by the animatronic. "Don't tell Daddy that I'm here. I wanted to watch your show, too. I don't know why he won't let me come see you. You're wonderful. Where did the other children go?"

WELCOME TO CIRCUS BABY'S PIZZA WORLD!

As the game begins, you start in an elevator, which descends for quite a while. Here you meet the Handyman's Robotics and Unit Repair System Model 5 (aka HandUnit). Think of HandUnit as your own personal Phone Guy. Your first task is to enter your name in the system, but no matter what you enter, it auto-corrects to "Eggs Benedict." When you get to the bottom, head toward the caution tape to crawl through the vent.

As you crawl, HandUnit explains that Freddy Fazbear's Pizza was a huge success until it was closed down, at which point there was room for a "new contender in children's entertainment." The animatronics at this location are rented out for parties; your job is to ensure they're in good working order.

NIGHT 1

Night 1 is fairly straightforward: Follow the directions offered by HandUnit to administer a "controlled shock" to Ballora and Funtime Foxy, which will summon them to their stages. Once they appear, crawl through the vent to the Circus Gallery Control Module to summon Circus Baby. She won't appear.

NIGHT 1

NIGHT 2

On your elevator ride, you can select a new voice for HandUnit. He gives you a few numbered options, but since there aren't any numbers on the keypad, you can't actually select a voice. Whatever button you press, it auto-corrects to "angsty teen."

In the Primary Control Module, follow HandUnit's instructions. Trying to summon Funtime Foxy and Ballora to the stage will cause a glitch, restoring HandUnit's default voice. Head through the vents to summon Circus Baby. This time, however, as you try to "motivate" Circus Baby, there's a power malfunction. HandUnit reboots the system, which also takes down the security doors, vent locks, and oxygen!

During the shutdown, you'll hear the voice of Circus Baby. She tells you to hide in a space under the desk that a previous guard created. Once under, pull on the metal sheet to close off the space. Moments later, you'll see BidyBab eyes peering through holes in the metal. Twice you'll need to pull the metal sheet shut as they tug on it. Failing to do so will result in a jump scare.

After the BidyBabs retreat, Circus Baby will start speaking once again, saying not to listen to HandUnit when it tells you to crawl through Ballora Gallery quickly. Instead, you should walk slowly and stop immediately if you hear music. Seconds later, HandUnit returns—the reboot of the system failed, and you'll need to restart it manually by crossing Ballora Gallery to the Breaker Room.

Ignore HandUnit's urging to speed up and advance across the gallery slowly. Stop completely if you hear Ballora's music get louder. Inside the Breaker Room, bring up the map of the building. Click and hold the buttons on the left side of the map to restore power to each area.

If you release the button before the power reaches 100 percent, it'll start to drop, but if you hold the button without listening for Funtime Freddy's approach, he'll attack. Try switching back and forth between the breaker screen and the room, playing audio to momentarily distract Freddy.

Once the breakers are back on, your shift is over. Exit through Ballora Gallery.

NIGHT 3

Your elevator trip tonight includes a musical selection! No matter what you type, you'll get "Casual Bongos." Tonight you're performing maintenance work on Funtime Freddy. You may not be qualified to do this, but that's okay—you'll be fine!

At the control center, check in on Ballora and Funtime Foxy. Ballora is on the stage in pieces. Funtime Foxy isn't there, but HandUnit doesn't notice. HandUnit tells you not to visit Circus Baby. When you're done, head into the right vent.

Freddy is in the Parts & Service Room on the other side of Funtime Auditorium, but to get to him you need to make it past Funtime Foxy. Unlike Ballora, who is triggered by sound, Funtime Foxy is motion activated. Her auditorium is dark, but you can use the flash beacon as needed. Once again, be patient and move in short bursts, flashing your light periodically. You'll be able to hear Foxy moving around in the dark; if you see him, stop and wait until she moves away.

When you reach the Parts & Service Room, HandUnit will give you instructions on how to open Freddy's face plate and chest cavity by clicking various buttons. Once the face plate and chest cavities are open, remove the power module and you're done with Freddy.

On to the Bon-Bon puppet . . . which has come to life and won't stop hiding behind Freddy. You'll need to collect the secondary power module by clicking the button just below Bon-Bon's bow tie. Since he'll just keep hiding from your flashlight until he ultimately jump-scares you, don't shine your light directly at him. Instead, wait for Bon-Bon to appear at the edge of the light; he'll start rising slowly from behind Freddy. When Bon-Bon's chest is visible, quickly click on the button to complete the repair.

You'll need to cross the Funtime Auditorium again on your way out. Don't worry about moving slowly—it's impossible to avoid triggering Funtime Foxy's jump scare, which ends the night.

NIGHT 4

No soaps tonight. When you awake, you're inside a spring lock suit, compliments of Circus Baby. She saved you . . . kidnapped you . . . whatever!

Shortly after two technicians bring Ballora into the Scooping Room, you get a front-row demonstration of the "Scooper" machine: In one fell scoop, it rips Ballora's endoskeleton straight out of her body.

After the men leave, Circus Baby opens the spring lock suit's face plates so that the company can find you on the security cameras and get you out of there. But you'll have to survive in the meantime.

There are ten spring locks in all—five on each side. Click and hold the spring locks to keep them wound, but beware the Minireenas that are closing in. You'll need to shake them off your suit before they climb up and jump-scare you. Note, however, that shaking them off causes the spring locks to unwind faster. Switch back and forth between these two tasks as quickly as possible, targeting the locks that are closest to being unwound while shaking off the incoming Minireenas.

NIGHT 5

To celebrate the end of your first week, the company is sending a gift basket! Type your preference into the keypad, though no matter what, you'll get Exotic Butters.

Heading toward the Primary Control Module, HandUnit reveals that there are still two technicians on site. When you check on Funtime Foxy and Ballora, you'll find them—hanging from the show stage.

Tonight you're performing maintenance on Circus Baby. Pass through the eerily empty Funtime Auditorium to reach her. When you enter the Parts & Service Room, you'll find Circus Baby deactivated, but you can still hear her voice. She tells you she's broken and that they want to scoop her, but she says that won't solve the problem. She asks you to save the good parts of her so that the bad will be destroyed.

Following her instructions, pull up Baby's hidden keypad and enter the code quickly and correctly. Failing to input the code correctly results in a jump scare by an endoskeleton. After opening the hatch on her arm, take the glowing green card and press the button on the conveyor belt.

As you send Circus Baby to be scooped, you can see the endoskeleton retreating into the darkness.

REAL ENDING

Follow Circus Baby's directions to get through Funtime Auditorium and reach the Scooping Room. HandUnit quickly reveals that you've entered a restricted area—you're on the wrong side of the Scooper.

Unfortunately, this was all part of Circus Baby's plan. As she explains, "If we looked like you, then we would have somewhere to go." You'll be able to catch a glimpse of a new animatronic in the window—Ennard—an amalgam of the animatronics you've met in this game. You'll find yourself powerless to prevent Ennard from "scooping" your insides out and replacing your skeleton with itself. Now Ennard can use your body to escape into the world.

As the credits roll, brightening up the image shows the text "REAL ENDING" in the lower left corner.

THE IMMORTAL AND THE RESTLESS

At the end of your shift each night, you'll get to watch a soap opera while munching popcorn. The show is called *The Immortal and the Restless*, and features a vampire named Vlad arguing with his mistress, Clara, about the paternity of their precocious baby, child support, etc. It's pretty obvious Vlad is the father . . . and that he and Clara are a bad match. Clara burns down his house, threatens to sell her ring, and more, but they ultimately reconcile.

Gameplay and Strategy

ANIMATRONICS INVENTORY: CIRCUS BABY

- Appearance: Similar to a circus clown with red hair in ponytails, rosy cheeks, and bright green eyes; wears a red skirt and cropped top with frills on the shoulders.

- While Circus Baby talks you through the bulk of the game, you only see her for a few minutes on Night 5.

ANIMATRONICS INVENTORY: BIDYBABS

- Appearance: Small, baby-doll-like animatronics with large eyes, triangular red noses, and square teeth.

- You'll spot the BidyBabs throughout the game—they try to pull you out from under the desk on Night 2, they're in the vent system during the custom night, and you can occasionally spot one in the elevator window.

- BidyBabs speak during Night 2 when you're hiding under the desk. Apparently they "always find a way inside" that crawl space.

ANIMATRONICS INVENTORY: FUNTIME FREDDY

♦ Appearance: Our favorite brown bear is now shiny white with light pink highlights. He's still got the tiny black hat, bow tie, buttons, and microphone.

♦ You'll first spot Funtime Freddy on Night 2 in the Breaker Room. On Night 3, you'll need to remove his power module in the Parts & Service Room.

♦ Freddy speaks to you creepily while you're working in the Breaker Room. His audio seems prerecorded and relates to kids and birthday parties, unlike Ballora and Circus Baby's audio, which is more complex.

ANIMATRONICS INVENTORY: BON-BON

♦ Appearance: On Funtime Freddy's hand is a puppet that looks very similar to Toy Bonnie: blue with light accents and a red bow tie.

♦ Bon-Bon plays "Mascot Response Audio" to get Funtime Freddy back on his stage in the Breaker Room. You can also hear his creepy giggles while trying to retrieve his power module in the Parts & Service Room.

ANIMATRONICS INVENTORY: BALLORA

♦ Appearance: A ballerina with painted white skin, rosy cheeks, blue hair, and a purple tutu.

♦ You can see Ballora from the Primary Control Module. You'll encounter her in Ballora Gallery on Night 2 and in the Scooping Room on Night 4.

♦ Ballora sings a creepy song on Night 2 if you listen closely . . .

ANIMATRONICS INVENTORY: MINIREENAS

♦ Appearance: Creepy, puppetlike dolls wearing tutus and white face masks that have two small eyeholes and a large mouth.

♦ Minireenas are first seen dancing alongside Ballora in the Ballora Gallery. They later appear to be holding up her animatronic parts after she's been scooped.

♦ You won't need to deal with Minireenas until Night 4, when you must "wiggle" to get them off your spring lock suit.

ANIMATRONICS INVENTORY: FUNTIME FOXY

♦ Appearance: Funtime Foxy has a similar color scheme to Funtime Freddy. The burnt-red fur has given way to a gleaming white and pink, with no eye patch or pirate's hook hand, just orange eyes.

♦ Funtime Foxy is located in the Funtime Auditorium and can be seen through the window in the Primary Control Module. You first encounter Funtime Foxy on Night 3 in the Funtime Auditorium.

♦ Funtime Foxy is motion activated, and features one of the few animatronic jump scares in the series that is required to advance to the next night.

ANIMATRONICS INVENTORY: ENNARD

♦ Appearance: Ennard is cobbled together from the endoskeletons of other animatronics—a complete mess of wires, springs, and metal . . . but at least it's wearing a fun party hat!

♦ Ennard shows up on Night 5; you'll see it for the first time through the window of the Scooping Room.

♦ If you look closely, you'll notice eyes placed in various spots on Ennard's body from the other animatronics.

Mapping the Animatronics and Special Events in FNAF Sister Location

Circus Gallery
Circus Baby is supposed to appear here.

Breaker Room
Funtime Freddy appears here.

Primary Control Module
Where the magic happens.

Ballora Gallery
Ballora appears here.

Elevators

FUNTIME AUDITORIUM
FUNTIME FOXY APPEARS HERE.

PRIVATE ROOM
ONLY ACCESSIBLE WITH CERTAIN STEPS.
SEE PAGES 134-136.

PARTS & SERVICE ROOM
FUNTIME FREDDY AND CIRCUS BABY APPEAR HERE.

SCOOPING ROOM

= FUNTIME FREDDY

= CIRCUS BABY

= FUNTIME FOXY

= ENNARD

= BALLORA

= MINIREENAS

= BON-BON

= BIDYBABS

Codes, Glitches, and Secrets

BLUEPRINTS

Perhaps the biggest secret in *Sister Location* is the blueprints for the four main animatronics (Circus Baby, Funtime Freddy, Ballora, and Funtime Foxy) found rarely on the game load screen. Though there is little chance that you'll encounter these blueprints outside the game's data files, you're missing out if you don't take a peek. They contain some pretty shocking revelations, and some of their design choices—all of which seem meant to lure children in to be kidnapped—are no doubt what the unnamed technicians were referencing in the Prologue.

A

C

D

Is that a kid in Freddy's storage tank??

Name: Funtime Fred
Height: 6.0 ft
Weight: 350 lbs

There is a very cool, very complicated secret ending to *Sister Location*, but to get there, we need to check a few boxes.

DON'T MISS THE BONUS CONTENT!

On Night 3, before heading to Funtime Auditorium, go to the Circus Gallery Control Room and enter the crawl space under the desk to hear a story from Circus Baby. She'll tell you about the first and only night she was on stage. Part of her programming requires her to count children. As soon as there was only one child left in the room with her, she lost control of herself. Her stomach opened and made an ice cream cone. Then she pulled the unfortunate child—a little girl—inside herself. Baby is still haunted by the little girl's screams.

C

B

A

D

Name: C

Height:

Weight:

A: Air Hos
B: Interna
    Dispens
C: Song Da
D: Emergen

t © xxxx Afton Robotics, LLC

FNAF·SL RETRO ARCADE

Circus Baby Mini-game

The Circus Baby mini-game may appear after a jump scare. In order to unlock the secret ending, you need to complete a task in this mini-game: Playing as Circus Baby, you must collect food and give it to children within a limited amount of time. Each kid needs to be fed two cupcakes, unless you hit them with a green cupcake. Their color will change from green to red when they've had their fill.

Collectible Food:
- **Pink Cupcake:** Single throw cupcakes
- **Blue Cupcake:** Triple throw; can feed kids lined up vertically
- **Green Cupcake:** Single throw; can fully feed multiple kids lined up horizontally
- **Ice Cream Cone:** Unlocks secret child

Jump to grab the pink cupcakes, and throw two at the first child and then another two at the next child. Continue right into the next area, but do *NOT* target the kids on the lower level! Instead, jump up and throw another two cupcakes each at the kids on the platforms.

From the upper-right platform, jump right into the next screen to leap over a blue cupcake and land on a middle island. Proceed right to the next area, and throw your last two pink cupcakes right as you jump to the first platform.

Return left to grab the blue cupcake, then head right again. Jump to the middle platform and throw twice to hit all three kids lined up vertically at the same time. Continue to the right, but do not grab the green cupcake. Hop onto the left edge of the platform to jump over it. In the next area, jump and throw twice to hit the three kids arranged vertically.

Now return left to collect the green cupcake. Continue left until you reach the area where you ignored the two unfed kids. Throw a green cupcake at them. Quickly return to the right, jumping all of the gaps. In the area where you hit the last set of three kids arranged vertically, there is a gap at the far end. Jump it, and immediately throw a cupcake to hit the kids in the next room! Continue to the right, jumping gaps and throwing cupcakes as necessary.

At the end of the screen, take the ice cream cone but *don't* exit to the GOAL. Instead, run all the way back to the left. You'll reach the end with only seconds to spare, but as long as the timer doesn't expire, a girl will come out for the ice cream. Circus Baby grabs her with a terrible scream.

To access the game quickly, go to the EXTRAS MENU AND MOVE YOUR MOUSE TO THE LOWER LEFT CORNER. CLICK ON THE ICON OF CIRCUS BABY WHEN IT APPEARS.

133

After successfully completing the Circus Baby mini-game, you can disobey Baby's directions on Night 5 as you head through Funtime Auditorium toward the Scooping Room. Moving to the right, you'll find the Private Room. HandUnit will inform you that you're not allowed to leave until 6:00 a.m. Sound familiar?

Yep! It's a challenge to survive the night against Ennard in a manner similar to FNAF. You've got doors to keep you safe, but limited power to keep them closed. Listen carefully for sound clues to determine Ennard's whereabouts and use the monitor sparingly. You know the drill.

After surviving the night, you'll be treated to a final installment of The Immortal and the Restless—complete with your "Exotic Butters" gift basket—but you're not alone. Ennard has followed you.

ENTER 1-9-8-3 ON THE KEYPAD TO BRING UP FNAF4 CAMERA FEEDS ON THE DESK MONITORS!

NOTICE THE FAMILIAR FREDBEAR PLUSH ON THE DESK.

CUSTOM NIGHT

Defeating Ennard unlocks a series of custom nights in the Private Room. Each night comes with preset AI difficulties, and you must defeat each night on "V. Hard" to access bonus cut scenes. The catch? Almost all the animatronics here are different, and each follows its own rules.

- **Ballora:** approaches from East or West Hall; close the door when her music gets louder.
- **Funtime Freddy/Bon-Bon:** hides in the closets outside either door; when he commands Bon-Bon to attack, close the corresponding door; if he shouts "surprise," close the opposite door.
- **Yenndo:** appears at random in the office; open the monitor to make him disappear.
- **Funtime Foxy:** sits in "Funtime Cove"; follows same rules as *FNAF* Foxy.
- **Bonnet:** rushes through your office; click on her nose to stop her.
- **BidyBab:** enters from the vent above your desk; close the vent when it gets too close.
- **Electrobab:** drains your power; administer a controlled shock to stop it.
- **Lolbit:** distracts you with audio and visuals; type L-O-L to stop it.
- **Minireenas:** drain your oxygen until you black out; administer a controlled shock to stop them.
- **Minireenas 2:** randomly appear over your line of sight; cannot be stopped.

NOTE THAT NONE OF THE CUSTOM NIGHT GAMEPLAY IS CONSIDERED CANON. (SORRY TO THE LOLBIT FANS.)

ON NIGHT 5, THE ENNARD MASK IN THE PRIMARY CONTROL MODULE IS MISSING, THOUGH IT WILL SOMETIMES CHANGE TO A LOLBIT MASK.

Foxy
t
lbs
ion Sen
Voice Sync
ght A
ele
hor
y d

CHECK OUT THE CREEPY PUPPETS IN THE CIRCUS GALLERY CONTROL ROOM.

Try clicking around the Primary Control Module. You can honk the masks' noses, make beeping sounds with the buttons, and more.

	Angry Ballet	Freddy & Co.	Funtime Frenzy	Dolls, Attack!	Girls' Night	Weirdos	Top Shelf	Bottom Shelf	Cupcake Challenge	Golden Freddy
Minireena 2	X				X	X			X	X
Minireena	X				X	X	X		X	X
Lolbit				X		X		X	X	X
Electrobab					X	X		X	X	X
Bidybab					X	X		X		X
Bonnet		X			X	X	X	X		X
Funtime Foxy		X	X		X		X		X	X
Yenndo		X	X			X	X			X
Funtime Freddy		X	X			X	X		X	X
Ballora	X				X		X		X	X

FINAL CUT SCENES

After defeating each of the first nine custom nights, you'll watch one of seven 8-bit cut scenes. Ennard (who now occupies your body) is going through the world like normal, only, your body is decaying. Ennard's endoskeleton eventually leaves in search of a fresher body, but strangely, your body comes back to life.

Defeating the Golden Freddy custom night unlocks something even more earth-shattering: this message from Michael.

"Father, it's me, Michael. I did it. I found it—it was right where you said it would be. They were all there. They didn't recognize me at first, but then they thought I was you. And I found her. I put her back together, just like you asked me to. She's free now. But something is wrong with me. I should be dead, but I'm not. I've been living in shadows. There is only one thing left for me to do now. I'm going to come find you. I'm going to come find you."

Lore and Theories

FAN THEORIES: A FAMILY AFFAIR

Many theorists insist that *Sister Location* proves that *FNAF* is truly a "family affair." Regardless of when the bite depicted in *FNAF4* happened, some theorists purport it introduces us to the family of William Afton.

THE YOUNGER SON: THE BITE VICTIM

William Afton seems to have been watching the bite victim in *FNAF4*, since the lighter areas of the Breaker Room map match up with the areas we explore/play in during *FNAF4*. Plus, the language at the close of the game that comes from plush Fredbear (who is shown holding a walkie-talkie in the Private Room) says, "I will put you back together." Sound familiar? It's the same thing Michael Afton says during the last custom night cut scene in *Sister Location*—I put her back together, just like you asked me to.

The Daughter: Circus Baby

At the end of each night in *Sister Location*, we overhear a girl pleading with her father to let her play with Circus Baby. On the final night, we hear that she is left alone with Circus Baby, and we know from Baby's dialogue on Night 3 that this only happened once. That time, she snatched and killed a little girl.

Michael Afton later tells his father that he found "her" and "put her back together"— could this be William Afton's daughter, Michael's sister? Theorists point to the Circus Baby mini-game for further proof. Prior to snatching the little girl in the game, Circus Baby's eyes are blue. In the present, her eye color matches that of the little girl from the mini-game—green.

The Older Son: Michael Afton, AKA, You

This is perhaps the only part of this theory that seems confirmed by the game. In the final cut scene, you call William Afton "father," and state your name—"Michael." (Remember how we saw "Mike" taped to the keypad in the elevator?) Strangely, in the 8-bit Ennard cut scene, when you come back to life, it's Circus Baby's voice— which theorists insist is your sister's voice—that seems to bring you back.

Fan Theories: Michael Afton is Not Purple Guy . . . Sort Of

Theorists believe that there may actually be two Purple Guys, positing that the Purple Guy who committed the murders in *FNAF* and appears in *FNAF2* and *4* is William Afton. He designed the animatronics to lure in children, so he seems to be the most likely suspect.

According to the theory, William's son Michael is the *other* Purple Guy we see in *FNAF3* and *Sister Location*. Michael, unfortunately, is simply a victim of mistaken identity. In the final *Sister Location* cut scene, Michael reveals that the animatronics "didn't recognize me at first, but then they thought I was you." If the animatronics mistook Michael for William Afton, then a whole lot of pieces fall into place.

Consider—Michael seems to be on a mission to "free" children's souls from the animatronics. It would make sense then that he would return to Fazbear's Fright to disinter the children's bodies from the animatronics. The trick is, when he disinters them, the children's souls are free to punish their murderer . . . and Michael looks *just like* the murderer—his own father. Michael is thus the Purple Guy inside Springtrap, and why Springtrap appears at the end of *Sister Location*.

Pretty interesting theory.

Eggs Benedict Recipe*

Ingredients required:
English muffins
Butter
Sliced Canadian bacon or ham
Distilled white vinegar
4 Eggs
Hollandaise sauce
Paprika

Directions:
Split and toast English muffins, and spread with butter. Brown Canadian bacon or ham in skillet using melted butter over medium heat.
Fill another skillet with 2-3 inches of water, and add four teaspoons of vinegar. Bring to a boil, then reduce to simmer. Break cold egg into a separate dish, then slip carefully into water. Cook 3-5 minutes until whites and yolks are firm. Place slices of Canadian bacon on each muffin half. Add egg. Spoon hollandaise sauce over eggs. Sprinkle paprika if desired.

* KIDS, ASK A PARENT TO HELP YOU!

HELLO
my name is

EGGS BENEDICT

Chapter 6

Freddy Fazbear's Pizzeria Simulator

CONGRATULATIONS! You, yes, you, have been chosen as the newest franchise owner of a Fazbear Entertainment restaurant! The sixth game in the Five Nights at Freddy's series, *Freddy Fazbear's Pizzeria Simulator*, puts you in the driver's seat of your very own restaurant. Choose the decor, the games, the entertainment; the possibilities are endless!

But it's not all fun and games. Split into three parts, the gameplay consists first of restaurant management, where you buy and place animatronics, games, and decor. The next stage is office maintenance, where hard-core *FNAF* fans are sure to shine. Your goal seems innocent enough: complete the tasks assigned to you in your dark office. But depending on your choices, you could find yourself fighting for your life against a horde of vicious animatronics, including some, er, not-so-friendly faces. The final part of your day is scrapping, where you must sort through and test old animatronics that were found outside your door to salvage them.

Pizzeria Simulator shocked and delighted fans with its new concept, allowing for near-infinite possibilities and a variety of different endings. Though first appearing as a fun and funny new take on the mythos of *FNAF*, the game quickly takes a dark turn. With creepy mini games that both answer old questions and open up new ones, and a "good" ending that seemingly wraps up some of the many mysteries of the franchise, *Pizzeria Simulator* is sure to keep you on your toes . . . and keep you up at night.

The Freddy Scoop

The game starts with an 8-bit mini game where, after you choose toppings for your own pizza, Freddy has to deliver pizzas to hungry customers. As the levels increase, a shadow Freddy will appear and try to block you from delivering the pizzas. As you continue to get past him, the game suddenly glitches, causing multiple shadow Freddys to appear until the screen cuts to black.

When the screen flickers back to life, you'll see Scrap Baby, a re-crafted version of Baby that escaped from Ennard. Look down to find a piece of paper and a tape recorder. The tape recorder plays and the Cassette Man asks you to document the responses of the animatronic based on various aural stimuli. Two noises play and seemingly nothing happens, so you can check "No," "Yes," or "Maybe" in each box. On the third test, the pitch of a creepy song rises and rises until the screen cuts to a training video.

The training video informs you that you are now a franchisee of Fazbear Entertainment. Congratulations! You'll be in charge of your very own pizzeria, which means you'll be required to buy equipment for entertainment purposes while also cutting costs to make a profit. Make sure not to cut too many costs, though, as you don't want to be liable for any "accidents."

DAY 1: MONDAY

From here you're taken to the Restaurant Management screen to buy equipment for your restaurant. Unfortunately, after buying the franchise license from Fazbear Entertainment, you only have $100 left. Your budget only allows you to choose items from the "Dumpster Diver Weekly" section, but there's still a lot to choose from. Each item has a different value for Atmosphere, Health & Sanitation, Entertainment, Bonus Revenue, and Liability. As you buy more expensive items, better categories such as "Stan's Budget Tech," "Smiles and Servos, Inc.," and "Rare Finds Auction" become available.

Once you're done purchasing, move on to the blueprint area to place the equipment in your restaurant. There's a blinking pink-and-blue icon in the top right corner inviting you to receive a "Sponsorship Offer," which means extra money for advertising a brand in your restaurant. You can also test the games you buy, which can help you receive bonus revenue.

THE PURPLE-
AND-WHITE
BEAR IS NAMED
"HELPY."

When you're happy with the restaurant, click "Finished!" in the bottom right corner to move to the next phase of the game: the office. Before you is a computer terminal. You must do all of your tasks before you can leave. Your tasks don't cost money to complete, but you can spend money to upgrade your equipment to make it quieter or more efficient. This is found in the Tasks screen and the Equipment subscreen.

Under the Tasks screen are several buttons: "Order Supplies," "Advertising," and "Maintenance." Click on a task to start completing it.

HONK THE NOSE ON THE HELPY DOLL ON TOP OF YOUR TERMINAL.

The Tutorial Unit warns that your terminal and ventilation system are very loud, so be sure to disable them if the noise is drawing unwanted attention to you. However, be careful about keeping the ventilation system off for too long, as the room will heat up.

To your left and right are open vents. You can keep track of what's going on in the vents by checking a motion detector, deploying an audio decoy, or using a secondary ventilation system. If all else fails, shining your flashlight into the vent will cause whatever is coming for you to retreat.

After finishing your tasks, you can log off. The Tutorial Unit congratulates you on a job well done, but reminds you that you must get through the full week in order to prove yourself. There's a big party this Saturday that you have to make it to, but if you are successful at that, you'll be rewarded.

Think you're done with your first day? Think again!

Welcome to the final phase of your day: salvaging. You're brought back to the dimly lit desk, a piece of paper and a recorder in front of you. Only this time you're facing Molten Freddy, a mess of parts from other animatronics that has donned a smashed Funtime Freddy mask.

Cassette Man tells you that you must inspect the animatronics that are found by the back door. No one knows why they're there, but they can be used for spare parts. You can either salvage them to make some extra money, or throw them away and lose revenue. Cassette Man informs you that if the animatronic attacks, you have the option to shock it. If you shock it more than three times, you will irreparably damage the hardware and the value will decrease.

If you fail to notice Molten Freddy's movements and you don't shock him, you will receive a jump scare and a notification: you lost the salvage, and now something is loose in your pizzeria.

Make it through all five stimuli, using your taser each time the animatronic moves, and you will receive money. As the screen cuts to black, a distorted voice is heard saying, "Thanks for letting me join the party. I'll try not to disappoint." The animatronic is still loose in your pizzeria.

The day ends with a summary screen totaling the amount of money you made from your restaurant for that day. Great job!

Summary		GREAT JOB!
New Visitors	20	
Returning Visitors	0	
Turned Away	0	
Total Visitors	20	
Food Revenue	$ 183	
Bonus Revenue	$ 0	
Salvage Revenue	$ 0	
Total Revenue	$ 183	

DAY 2: TUESDAY

Welcome back! You're brought to the Restaurant Management screen again, where you now have the option to buy more advanced equipment thanks to yesterday's profits. The more expensive items you buy, the more categories you can buy from. Watch out for the liability ratings on the animatronics and other robots, particularly the warnings that there might be something undesirable hiding inside.

Choose what you like and then you're brought to the Blueprint screen, where you can place your items. You can also modify what you've bought by adding coin slots for bonus revenue, cleaning and polishing the item for extra atmosphere, or adding safety straps to reduce risk. Another opportunity presents itself to receive a sponsorship, making you even more money than last time!

MAKE SURE TO PURCHASE CANDY CADET, AS HE MAY GIVE YOU A SURPRISE! (SEE PAGE 160.)

Once finished, you're brought back to your office. Remember to complete your tasks as fast as you can while also monitoring the air vents to your left and right.

WARNING: If you salvaged an animatronic or purchased any of the high-liability animatronics, they will come for you through the vents.

You can pause a task on the computer screen, or shut down your computer terminal completely if you hear a noise and need to check the vents. The animatronics are attracted to sound, so use an audio decoy to distract them. You'll also need to monitor the temperature in the room, though the fans and vents can be pretty loud.

WARNING: If you took a sponsorship, your tasks will be interrupted by a loud advertisement that will play on your terminal.

If you complete your tasks and avoid a jump scare, you're brought to the Salvage screen again, where you can choose to salvage Scraptrap, or throw it away. If you salvage successfully, Scraptrap can be heard saying, "What a deceptive calling. I knew it was a lie the moment I heard it, obviously. But it is intriguing nonetheless . . ."

The Tutorial Unit reminds you, "Don't forget: Saturday, you want them to all be in one place!"

Day 3: Wednesday

Halfway there! You're once more brought to the Restaurant Management and Blueprint screens. Note that you can upgrade the size of your restaurant to accommodate more items, or take another sponsorship to earn more cash.

Buy and test the arcade games Midnight Motorist and Fruity Maze for a special surprise!

(See pages 162-164.)

Now back to the office! If you attempted to salvage both animatronics, you'll notice things have gotten a little harder. Complete your tasks without dying and you're brought to the Salvage screen, where you can choose to salvage Scrap Baby, whom you saw at the beginning of the game. If you salvage successfully, you can hear her say, "You don't really know your employer, do you?" as the screen cuts to black.

Depending on what you bought and the liability issues associated with the equipment, you might find yourself presented with several lawsuits on the Summary screen that you can choose to either fight or settle.

Summary	
New Visitors	20
Returning Visitors	0
Turned Away	0
Total Visitors	20
Food Revenue $	183
Bonus Revenue $	0
Salvage Revenue $	0
Total Revenue $	183
New Lawsuits	1

SETTLE	$	900
LEGAL FEES (fight lawsuit)	$	475
NEXT		

$ 283

1 / 1

DAY 4: THURSDAY

Another day, another dollar! You're brought back to the Management screen, where you can continue to buy equipment and change the blueprint of your restaurant, upgrading as you see fit. The office will get even more difficult if you salvaged Scrap Baby.

IF YOU'RE ABLE TO MAKE ENOUGH MONEY THROUGH SALVAGING, SPONSORSHIPS, AND BONUS REVENUE FROM TESTING YOUR PRODUCTS, PURCHASE THE SECURITY PUPPET FOR A SURPRISE! (SEE PAGE 165.)

Security Puppet $ 12500

Item condition: Very Good

On tonight's Salvage screen, you're presented with Lefty. If you purchased him from the store, you'll be presented with a sign of a winking smiley face that says, "No one is here. I'm already inside," with the only option being to throw it back in the alley. You know the drill; if you choose to salvage him, tase Lefty every time he moves, but not more than three times or you'll reduce his value.

DAY 5: FRIDAY

Keep on keeping on. Buy all the new things! Blueprint those things! Be careful in your office. Lucky you - no salvages today!

DAY 6: SATURDAY

Go about your business filling your restaurant with all the goodies your money can buy. Move along to the office and stay alive through your tasks.

REAL ENDING

After you complete your tasks for the night, the screen goes dark and you'll hear Scrap Baby's voice: "You played right into our hands . . . You gathered them all together in one place, just like he asked you to. All of those little souls in one place. Just for us. A gift. Now we can do what we were created to do and be complete . . ."

Cassette Man interrupts Scrap Baby, calling her Elizabeth. He explains that all the animatronics carrying trapped souls have been brought here and sealed inside as the restaurant is set on fire. Scrap Baby, Scraptrap, Lefty, and Molten Freddy are shown burning as they try to escape, along with images of the various 8-bit mini games from past *FNAF* games.

Cassette Man further states that the restaurant was made to lure the animatronics inside and destroy them so the souls can be freed. All except for one. "The darkest pit of Hell has opened to swallow you whole, so don't keep the Devil waiting, old friend," he says as Scraptrap burns.

Addressing the player, he goes on to say that he had designated an escape route for you, but has a feeling you don't want to leave. Lastly, Cassette Man talks to his daughter and apologizes for not being able to save her.

As the feed cuts out, you're presented with a new voice-over, congratulating you with a certificate of completion.

Gameplay and Strategy

Money Money Money

♦ Use all ten tokens you're given each day to test out your games in the pizzeria. You make bonus revenue if you perform well in the mini games!

The Office

♦ Monitor the motion sensor carefully and watch out for the blips on the screen. That's where the animatronics are!

♦ Use the audio decoy to move animatronics away from you. But make sure you're employing the decoy within the circular audio range; otherwise the animatronic won't hear it!

♦ Listen closely so you can distinguish between the sounds of animatronics entering the hall, entering the vent, and shuffling out of the vent!

Don't Tase Me!

♦ Remember that the animatronics won't move while you're looking at them. They only move when you hold up the piece of paper to check off their responses. If the animatronic is suddenly sitting upright, shock it!

Mapping Animatronics and Tips in Freddy Fazbear's Pizzeria Simulator

This is the safest place to play an audio cue, as it's the farthest from you.

This big square is the restaurant.

= Molten Freddy

= Scrap Baby

= Lefty

= Scraptrap

You are here.

You will hear audio cues from each of the animatronics when they are in these vents.

Animatronics can take any path to you!

ANIMATRONICS INVENTORY: MOLTEN FREDDY

- Appearance: He's certainly not the Freddy we've come to love and fear. A tangle of wires with a variety of eyeballs poking out at random, Molten Freddy is all razor-sharp teeth in a rusted metal face. You want to feel sorry for him . . . until he tries to kill you, that is.

- Molten Freddy is worth $500 and can be salvaged on the first night, unless you buy the Discount Ball Pit on Monday. If you do, a wooden sign appears in his usual chair, hinting that he's made his way into the restaurant by hiding in the ball pit. He doesn't make any particular sound as he climbs through the vents, nor does he speak to you when he's in the vents.

ANIMATRONICS INVENTORY: SCRAPTRAP/WILLIAM AFTON

- Appearance: Similar to Springtrap, Scraptrap is a yellowish rabbit, though he's considerably more worn and damaged, with holes throughout his body and wires poking out. His top jaw shows off buckteeth, with pointed fangs on his bottom jaw. With a severed forearm, no ears, and some suspiciously human-looking parts beneath his fur, Scraptrap is certainly a sight to behold.

- Scraptrap appears on the second night and is worth $1,000. If you purchase the Nedd Bear animatronic on Tuesday, Scraptrap won't appear, implying that he hides inside the other animatronic during the day. Scraptrap is one of the most vocal enemies. As he approaches you from the vents, you can hear him saying, "You may not recognize me at first, but I assure you, it's still me." He also makes a loud clamoring sound as he makes his way toward you.

ANIMATRONICS INVENTORY: SCRAP BABY

- Appearance: Compared to the Circus Baby of *Sister Location*, Scrap Baby has orange, silver, and red pigtails with more realistic strands of hair, along with a new outfit that includes coiled sleeves on her arms. Scrap Baby's face and chest expose her wiring, and her right hand has been replaced with the claw that was once inside her stomach.

- Scrap Baby can be salvaged on the third night and is worth $2,000. As she approaches the vents to jump-scare you in your office, she can be heard saying, "I heard your call!" and "It feels like . . . my birthday. Did you have a gift for me?"

ANIMATRONICS INVENTORY: LEFTY

- Appearance: Also known as Lure Encapsulate Fuse Transport Extract, *Lefty* is the only animatronic that can be both bought and salvaged in *Pizzeria Simulator*. His body and features are similar to Toy Freddy from *FNAF2*, although his fur is dark gray and he wears a red top hat and bow tie. He also has a gold star on his chest like the other Rockstar animatronics. His jaw is open and held up with metal poles, and his left eye is black. He holds a microphone in his left hand. Onstage, Lefty dances erratically, setting him apart from the non-possessed animatronics.

- Lefty can either be bought for $5 with a liability rating of 9, the highest of any piece of equipment, or salvaged on the fourth night for $5,000. Similar to Molten Freddy, he doesn't speak when he is in the vents.

Codes, Glitches, and Secrets

ADDITIONAL CERTIFICATES

Certificate of Mediocrity:
If you refrain from buying or salvaging anything in the course of playing the game, you are awarded this certificate and the "lazy" ending and are fired from the restaurant.

Certificate of
Mediocrity

Certificate of Bankruptcy:
If you run out of money by the end of the game by purchasing expensive equipment or incurring lots of lawsuits, you are awarded this certificate and fired from the restaurant.

Certificate of
Bankruptcy

Blacklisted Certificate:
If you end the game with a risk rating of fifty or higher and win (i.e., you don't go bankrupt), you're awarded this certificate and can never work for a Fazbear Entertainment establishment ever again.

You Have Been
Blacklisted

Certificate of Insanity:
Start by buying Egg Baby (Data Archive) from the Restaurant Management screen and placing it in your restaurant.

Go through the rest of the game as usual and then head to your office. The button on your computer terminal should have switched from gray to blue. Turn off the monitor by pressing "Z," then click and hold the power button on the monitor, and press "Z" again. An audio file plays called HRY223. You're greeted with secret blueprints of several animatronics and devices.

You learn that the Scooper from *Sister Location* infuses things with soul energy, or "remnant." Remnant can be destroyed by overheating.

You also learn that Molten Freddy still contains the souls of Ballora, Funtime Freddy, and Funtime Foxy.

The final blueprint reveals that Lefty is an acronym, which stands for "Lure Encapsulate Fuse Transport & Extract." Lefty was created by Henry to lure and capture The Puppet with a specific frequency using a bracelet code.

Lorekeeper Certificate:
As the only certificate that isn't tied to an ending, this one is earned by playing all three mini games that are associated with lore. If you unlock the secrets of Midnight Motorist, Fruity Maze, and Security Puppet, and get the "real ending," you're not only awarded this certificate on the Start screen after you end the game, but you also earn a secret ending screen after the credits roll.

Candy Cadet:

If you spend a token on Candy Cadet, there's a chance he may reveal a secret story to you!

♦ The first story is about a young woman who is sealed in a small room and given five keys. She is told that each room opens the door to a child, but she can save only one. She melts the keys into one key, hoping to save all five. Unfortunately, the key now opens none of the doors and all the children die.

♦ The second story is about a boy who owns a hungry snake. One day he finds five kittens and keeps them in a shoe box. Each night for five nights, the snake sneaks out of its cage and eats a kitten. Filled with regret, the boy cuts open the snake and sews together the remains of the five kittens, putting them back in the shoe box.

♦ The last story is about a kind man who adopted five orphans to protect them from the world. While the man is away, a criminal breaks into his home and kills the children. The man can afford only one coffin, so he stitches the children together to form one body. That night, there was a knock at the door . . .

Egg Baby (Data Archive):

The name of the audio file you receive when buying Egg Baby is "HRY223," which theorists believe to be a reference to Henry, William Afton's partner and the father of Charlotte/Charlie in the *FNAF* book series.

GRAVESTONES:

If you play the Midnight Motorist, Fruity Maze, and Security Puppet games and receive the Lorekeeper Certificate, you're rewarded at the end of the credits with a rare screen of a series of graves in a flowering meadow. The names on the graves are Gabriel, Fritz, Susie, and Jeremy—whom fans believe to be the victims of the original killings. One of the graves is hidden from view. The last grave is on the hill in the background. Some fans believe that grave says "Charlie" or "Charlotte" on it, implying that Henry's daughter is watching over the children who were killed by William Afton, just as the Puppet watched over them. The hidden grave is said by fans to be Golden Freddy. To uncover more secrets, read the Five Nights at Freddy's *Survival Logbook!*

THE END

PICKLES:

As the only item in the entire Restaurant Management Catalog with a "Happiness" rating, these elusive devils are unfortunately "sold out" for the entire duration of the game. So how can you go about unlocking them? First, buy all the items in the catalog and then unlock the "Posh Pizzeria" achievement badge (see page 168). After that, the pickles are purchasable for $15! Enjoy!

Midnight Motorist

During the fourth lap of Midnight Motorist, hit other cars to slow down, then drive across to the bottom lane. Eventually you'll see there is an opening at the bottom of the screen you can enter.

You'll be led to another screen, where it's raining and you're just one purple car driving along a winding road. As you drive to the U-shaped bend in the road, crash your car into the dark clearing in the trees. You can get out (you'll find that your character is yellow, not purple!) and walk to an open spot in the trees. In the upper left corner there's an unmarked pile of dirt.

Get back in your car and you'll reach a fork in the road where you can either go left or continue straight. If you turn left, you're brought to a parking lot where there's a restaurant called JR's. There's a green man standing outside the restaurant. Park and get out of the car.

As you approach the green man, he says, "Come on, you know you can't be here. Don't make this more difficult than it has to be." Nothing else happens.

FFPS RETRO ARCADE

Get back in your car and turn right. Keep driving until you reach a blue house. You can get out of your car and walk around the house. The sound of music fades away and is replaced with the sound of rain. The closer you get to the house, the more it zooms in on your character. Go to the front door and enter the house. The game falls silent. There's a person dressed in gray sitting in a chair in front of a TV. The gray person says, "Leave him alone tonight. He had a rough day."

Go down the hall and knock on the door. You'll shout, "I told you not to close your door." Then, "This is my house. He can't ignore me like that." Then "OPEN THE DOOR," and finally, "I'll find a way in from outside."

Leave the house and walk around to the back. The window is broken and there are two sets of footprints, one human and one animatronic. Your character says: "Ran off to that place again. He'll be sorry when he gets back."

Fruity Maze

On the first level, hit a magnet to attract nearby fruits and a big purple slug to walk through walls. Collect all the fruits before the time runs out to advance to the next level. You'll see a reflection in the screen of a happy blonde girl.

As you start the second level, the music sounds slowed down. This time you're collecting bloodied dogs along with fruits. Now when the screen flashes, the little girl is frowning.

As you start the third and final round, you're collecting dead dogs, flowers, and white boxes. You leave behind bloody footprints as you walk. The music is slowed down even more and you'll find you can't use any magnets or slug power-ups. As the screen flashes, you'll see the girl crying with Spring Bonnie lurking behind her.

Suddenly, a car horn starts honking. Time ended! The game disappears and the text on the screen reads, "He's not really dead . . . ," "He is over here," and "Follow me . . ." as the screen starts flickering.

FFPS RETRO ARCADE

Security Puppet

You're brought to a screen with directions to not let your assigned child reach the exit. Your child's code is green. Near the exit there's a large purple-and-white wrapped present. Every now and then the lid lifts up and the Puppet's green eyes peek out. After a couple of rounds pass with no sight of a child with a green armband, the screen cuts to black.

Next, the game opens and a child wearing the green armband is outside in the rain, looking in the window. There's another box on top of the purple one. Suddenly, the Puppet leaps out of the purple box and floats toward the child at the window.

The Puppet exits the building in the rain. The Puppet keeps walking, but then slumps over. Eventually its green eyes die out and it becomes grayer and grayer as it short-circuits. The Puppet drags itself forward. There's a gray child on the ground. The Puppet slumps over and dies holding the child.

Throw it back
into the alley.

RARE SCREENS

In addition to the Gravestones screen mentioned on page 161, the Springtrap/Little Blonde Girl screen after the third round of Fruity Maze, and the "I'm already inside" screen you get during salvaging if the animatronics have already entered the restaurant, there are four rare screens showing the main antagonist animatronics waiting to be salvaged in the alleyway.

Molten Freddy is seen here resembling Ennard from *Sister Location*. He's made up mostly of a tangle of wires, and you can also spot a yellow-orange eye that belongs to Funtime Foxy, a magenta eye belonging to Bon-Bon, a blue eye belonging to Funtime Freddy, and a purple eye belonging to Ballora.

Scrap Baby is seen here with three posters behind her on the wall in the alleyway. One is of a clown laughing and two contain text that appears to be a contract. The most intriguing is what appears to be the "Twisted Wolf" from the *FNAF* novel *The Twisted Ones*.

Scraptrap's rare screen shows him slumped over in the alleyway with four posters behind him. Similar to Scrap Baby's, there appear to be two posters of contract pages. The other two posters depict a Halloween "Spook-Fest" and a building with gargoyle lions flanking a set of stairs. Perhaps these are allusions to Springtrap's introduction in *FNAF3*?

Lefty's rare screen has sparked the most fan theories. Some fans suggest the poster behind Lefty represents William Afton and his children. William would be the elderly ventriloquist; Michael, the talking dummy who looks identical to the old man; Elizabeth, who is believed to possess Circus Baby, is the clown; and the bear with the razor-sharp teeth is the third Afton child, considered by many to be the bite victim from *FNAF4*. Examining Lefty's right arm, you can spot a thin striped appendage reminiscent of the Puppet. The poster farthest to the right depicts a Puppet face as well, hinting at the fact that the Puppet is trapped inside of Lefty. (See page 169.)

Achievement Badges

Trash and the Gang

Unlock the "Trash and the Gang" achievement badge by buying the Deluxe Concert Stage and the Star Curtain Stage along with the five "trash" animatronics. Place Bucket Bob on the Star Curtain Stage and the rest on the Deluxe Concert Stage.

Unlock the "Mediocre Melodies" achievement badge by buying the Deluxe Concert Stage, the Star Curtain Stage, and the five cheaper animatronics. Place Orville Elephant on the Star Curtain Stage and the rest on the Deluxe Concert Stage.

Mediocre Melodies

Rockstars Assemble

Unlock the "Rockstars Assemble" achievement badge by buying the Deluxe Concert Stage the Star Curtain Stage, and the five Rockstar animatronics. Place Lefty on the Star Curtain Stage and the rest on the Deluxe Concert Stage.

Unlock the "Posh Pizzeria" achievement badge by buying the Deluxe Concert Stage (no need for the Star Curtain stage) and the three most expensive animatronics.

Posh Pizzeria

Purchase and play Prize King to win Funtime Chica at no additional cost.

Lore and Theories

FAN THEORIES: THE END OF FNAF?

With the destruction of the possessed animatronics, *Pizzeria Simulator* seems to mark the end of an era for *FNAF*, and fans had a lot to say about that ending.

Many fans theorize that Cassette Man is actually Henry, inventor of the animatronics and original partner of William Afton. Henry collects the possessed animatronics to burn them, which, according to the blueprints found in Egg Baby, is the only way to free the souls trapped inside the animatronics. But whose spirits are they?

Fans figured out that Scraptrap is William Afton and Scrap Baby is his daughter Elizabeth, as mentioned by Cassette Man at the end of the game. Rare screens seem to confirm that Ennard is disguising himself as Molten Freddy, while Lefty has the Puppet inside him. Some fans have gone on to suggest that the Puppet is Henry's daughter, Charlotte. As shown in the blueprints from the Egg Baby Data Archive, Lefty's job is to lull children and capture them, which he likely did to the Puppet, whom fans believe Charlotte is possessing.

Some fans have even gone on to suggest that the trap containing the animatronics at the end of *Pizzeria Simulator* is representative of the infamous locked box from *FNAF4*, alluding to the recurring theme mentioned in Candy Cadet's secret stories of five being made into one that are kept in a box.

But is it really over? We've seen Springtrap burn before in *FNAF3* . . . so is the FNAF series finished, as some fans believe? We doubt it.

Fan Theories: Mini Games Show the Original Killings

Perhaps the place where the most lore is uncovered is the mini games, which can be purchased in the Restaurant Management Catalog.

Fruity Maze

In Fruity Maze, you're shown flashes of a blonde girl smiling as she collects fruits. In the next levels, she gradually gets sadder as she collects dead and dying dogs. Some fans theorize that this girl is one of the original kidnapping victims, whose name appears on one of the gravestones at the end of the game.

Another popular theory posits that Mangle from *FNAF2* is the girl's dog! Fans believe the girl's dog died and she was lured away by William Afton to watch him reanimate it as an animatronic. Fans point to the fact that the dog in the game is missing an eye, like Mangle, and that Mangle is unlike other animatronics in that it doesn't speak, only making gargled radio noises.

MIDNIGHT MOTORIST

Midnight Motorist surprised fans by revealing that the driver of the purple car was yellow instead of the much-anticipated Purple Guy. Some have theorized that the yellow guy is still William Afton and that the gray person watching TV in the house is his son Michael. The runaway son is believed to be the bite victim, who was stolen by the animatronic, as there were two sets of footprints—one human and one animatronic—leading away from the broken window.

Another interesting theory posits that the yellow man isn't Afton at all, but the father of one of the kidnapping victims. The animatronic footprints were made by Afton, wearing the Spring Bonnie suit, who broke into the house and stole the child from his bed.

Other theories have also popped up around the secret grave in the clearing, with many fans linking it to the Twisted animatronics from *The Twisted Ones* novel, who would bury themselves to hide during the day.

Some fans theorize that the Security Puppet mini game portrays the death of Henry's daughter, Charlotte. While she waited outside in the rain in the green armband, they believe she was captured and murdered by William Afton (as shown in *FNAF2*'s "Take Cake to the Children" mini game, Page 45) and her body was thrown in the alleyway. When the Security Puppet went outside to try to save her and short-circuited, it died holding her, allowing her spirit to enter the Puppet and take over.

Chapter 7

ULTIMATE CUSTOM NIGHT

You asked for it, you got it! Ultimate Custom Night is the seventh and arguably most difficult of the FNAF games to date.

You're once again stuck in an office with murderous animatronics, but this time, there are more than fifty of them roaming the building and they each have their own way of attacking, distracting, and annoying you! Lucky for you, you can set their difficulty from zero to twenty and decide whom you want to fight, or have a go at one of sixteen themed challenges. As you rack up points, you unlock cut scenes and lore, possibly relating to who you are and what you're doing.

From your office you need to keep an eye on doors, vents, and air hoses that allow those pesky animatronics to get in. You also need to monitor the heater, air-conditioning, music box, and power generator, as well as the camera, ventilation, and air duct systems. (You know, for those animatronics that are heat or sound sensitive.)

But don't worry, you'll learn on your feet. At least you get a Freddy mask and a flashlight! Don't forget to set those laser traps in the vents, purchase items from the Prize Counter, and watch those Pirate Cove curtains closely, all while collecting Faz-Coins.

Like we said: you asked for it.

The Freddy Scoop

Gameplay begins with the character screen, where you have the option to set fifty animatronics to difficulty levels ranging from zero to twenty. On the sidebar you have the option to set them all to zero, five, ten, or twenty, or to add one individually. You can also see how many points you would receive for a perfect score based on the difficulty of the animatronics. The game will record your highest score along with your best time for that particular difficulty setting. When you've made your selections, press "Go!"

You're greeted by the Controls screen, which will help you react quickly to the various animatronics. Press "Go!" when you're ready to be brought to your office. There are doors on your left and right, along with a vent in front of you and to your right. There are also two duct hoses coming down from the ceiling.

Your job is to fight off the animatronics, which differ in number and difficulty based on your character settings. This means the gameplay will change for every setting but the controls remain the same.

HONK THE NOSE OF THE LITTLE FREDDY FAZBEAR ON YOUR DESK

Gameplay and Strategy

YOUR BASIC SCREEN shows you the number of Faz-Coins you have in the top left corner, your power usage and percentage along with noise level in the bottom left corner, the time in the top right corner, and the temperature in the bottom right corner.

YOUR POWER INDICATOR appears in the bottom left corner of your screen, showing how much power you have left, and how much power you're using. The ventilation and monitor consume the most power. You can turn the ventilation off until the temperature reaches eighty, but you will attract heat-sensitive animatronics. Also, don't forget that the ventilation system needs to be reset every thirty seconds!

Number of power bars	Average time it takes to drain 1%	Power drained per hour
Idle	10 seconds	4.5%
1	3 seconds	15%
2	1.25 seconds	36%
3	0.75 seconds	64.29%
4	0.5 seconds	90%
5	0.33 seconds	136%
6	0.25 seconds	180%

The longer the doors and vents are shut, the more power you lose. While you can't get power back, you can potentially receive a booster the more often you play (even if you lose), or by clicking on Rockstar Foxy's parrot, which will summon him and offer you one of four power-ups, including one percent more power. The only way to slow down power consumption is to use the additional power generator, which can be activated by pulling up your monitor and clicking on the "Power Generator" button in the top right of your screen. But be careful—the generator causes a lot of noise.

YOUR MONITORING SYSTEM is activated by swiping down on the right white arrow at the bottom of your screen. There you can monitor the camera, ventilation, and duct systems. You can also reset or silence the ventilation, enable the power generator, enable the heater or air-conditioning, and turn on the global music box.

THE CAMERA SYSTEM shows eight cameras used to monitor the animatronics.

THE VENTILATION SYSTEM shows a small icon of any animatronics that are in the vents. You can deploy vent snares to trap certain animatronics. If there's not enough oxygen, you will need to reset the ventilation.

THE DUCT SYSTEM shows a series of colored caution symbols that correspond to the animatronics in the ducts. You can close only one duct at a time, or you can set an audio lure or turn on the heat to push the animatronics back.

NOISE LEVEL AND TEMPERATURE go hand in hand. Everything that cools or heats the office causes noise, and everything that stops noise makes the temperature rise. The noise can be monitored in the bottom left corner, the temperature in the bottom right. Almost every action makes noise temporarily, including closing the doors.

Collect **FAZ-COINS** by clicking on them as they appear on the cameras or by asking Rockstar Foxy. Coins are also awarded as a power-up at the beginning of the game, depending on how often you play and what bonuses you achieve. Keep track of your coins in the top left corner of your screen.

THE DEATH COIN can be purchased for ten Faz-Coins on Camera 7, but can be used only once per night. It allows you to eliminate certain animatronics without removing points.

THE GLOBAL MUSIC BOX soothes certain animatronics. It doesn't change your noise level, but increases power consumption.

THE FREDDY MASK is enabled by swiping down on the left, reddish arrow and prevents jump scares from certain animatronics.

BONUSES appear to you after every game played, regardless of performance.

 "Frigid" allows you to start playing at a temperature of fifty degrees.

 "3 Coins" allows you to start the game with three Faz-Coins.

 "Battery" gives you bonus power, totaling 102 percent.

 "Dee Dee Repel" prevents Dee Dee and her friends from appearing during the game. Does not work in 50/20 mode where Dee Dee is replaced with XOR.

POINTS AND TROPHIES

Point totals must be accumulated to unlock "Intermissions," office skins, and trophies.

An intermission appears for every 700 points earned. These include Toy Chica: The High School Years, Bear of Vengeance, and a twitching Golden Freddy.

Office skins can also be unlocked. The *Sister Location* skin costs 2,000 points, the *FNAF3* skin costs 5,000, and the *FNAF4* skin costs 8,000.

You can also receive three trophies in bronze, silver, and gold if you win against a certain number of animatronics cranked up to 20 difficulty. Bronze is awarded for winning 40/20 mode, silver for 45/20 mode, and gold for 50/20 mode.

CHALLENGES

There are sixteen official challenges within the game, which can help you achieve more points and unlock cut scenes.

	Bears Attack 1	Bears Attack 2	Bears Attack 3
Freddy	10	10	20
Golden Freddy	1	10	10
Phantom Freddy	1	5	10
Nightmare Fredbear	10	10	20
Nightmare	10	10	20
Helpy	1	10	5
Nedd Bear	1	10	10
Rockstar Freddy	5	10	10
Molten Freddy	1	10	10
Lefty	1	10	10
Toy Freddy	0	1	5
Nightmare Freddy & Freddles	0	5	10

	Pay Attention 1	Pay Attention 2
JJ	5	20
The Puppet	5	10
Nightmare BB	5	20
Old Man Consequences	5	10
Funtime Foxy	5	10
Helpy	10	20
Music Man	10	20
El Chip	5	10
Funtime Chica	10	20
Scraptrap	5	20
Phone Guy	10	20
Balloon Boy	0	20

	Creepy Crawlies 1	Creepy Crawlies 2
Mangle	10	20
Withered Chica	5	20
Withered Bonnie	10	20
Marionnette	5	10
Springtrap	10	20
Phantom Mangle	5	10
Ennard	10	20
Happy Frog	5	20
Mr. Hippo	5	20
Pigpatch	5	20
Nedd Bear	5	20
Orville Elephant	5	20
Music Man	5	10
Molten Freddy	5	20
Scraptrap	0	1

	Ladies Night 1	Ladies Night 2	Ladies Night 3
Chica	5	5	10
Toy Chica	5	10	20
Mangle	5	5	10
JJ	1	5	10
Withered Chica	5	10	20
Jack O' Chica	5	10	20
Circus Baby	1	5	10
Ballora	1	5	10
Happy Frog	5	10	20
Rockstar Chica	1	5	10
Funtime Chica	1	5	10
Scrap Baby	1	5	10
Nightmare Mangle	0	1	10
Funtime Foxy	0	0	10

SPRINGTRAPPED

20	JJ
20	Springtrap
20	Phantom Mangle
20	Phantom Freddy
20	Phantom BB
10	Nightmarionne
10	Trash and the Gang
20	Rockstar Foxy
20	Scraptrap
20	Lefty

NIGHTMARES ATTACK

20	Withered Bonnie
20	Golden Freddy
20	Nightmare Freddy
20	Nightmare Bonnie
20	Nightmare Fredbear
20	Nightmare
20	Jack O' Chica
20	Nightmare Mangle
20	Nightmarionne
20	Nightmare BB
20	Music Man
20	Molten Freddy
20	Scrap Baby
20	Lefty

OLD FRIENDS

20	Freddy
20	Bonnie
20	Chica
20	Foxy
20	Toy Freddy
20	Toy Bonnie
20	Toy Chica
20	Mangle
20	BB
20	The Puppet
20	Springtrap
20	Circus Baby
20	Phone Guy

CHAOS 1

Toy Freddy	5
Withered Bonnie	5
The Puppet	5
Phantom Mangle	5
Nightmare Freddy	5
Nightmare Fredbear	5
Nightmare	5
Jack O' Chica	5
Old Man Consequences	5
Ballora	5
Trash and the Gang	1
Helpy	5
Happy Frog	1
Mr. Hippo	1
Pigpatch	1
Rockstar Freddy	5
Rockstar Bonnie	5
Rockstar Foxy	5
Music Man	5
El Chip	5
Funtime Chica	5
Scraptrap	5

CHAOS 2

Freddy	5
Toy Bonnie	5
Toy Chica	5
The Puppet	10
Golden Freddy	10
Phantom Freddy	20
Phantom BB	10
Nightmare Bonnie	10
Nightmare Mangle	5
Old Man Consequences	10
Circus Baby	5
Trash and the Gang	10
Helpy	10
Happy Frog	5
Mr. Hippo	5
Pigpatch	5
Rockstar Freddy	5
Rockstar Chica	5
Rockstar Foxy	10
Music Man	20
El Chip	10
Funtime Chica	10
Scrap Baby	20
Scraptrap	20
Phone Guy	10

CHAOS 3

Bonnie	20
Foxy	20
Toy Bonnie	5
Toy Chica	5
Mangle	5
Balloon Boy	5
JJ	5
Withered Chica	5
Withered Bonnie	20
Phantom Mangle	20
Phantom BB	20
Nightmare Bonnie	20
Nightmarionne	20
Nightmare BB	20
Old Man Consequences	20
Ennard	20
Trash and the Gang	20
Helpy	20
Happy Frog	10
Mr. Hippo	10
Pigpatch	10
Nedd Bear	20
Orville Elephant	20
Rockstar Freddy	10
Rockstar Bonnie	20
Rockstar Chica	20
Rockstar Foxy	20
Music Man	20
El Chip	20
Funtime Chica	20
Lefty	20
Phone Guy	20

ANIMATRONICS INVENTORY: FREDDY

- Approaches from the left hall, progressing in stages toward your door. Keep track of him on the monitor and shut the door when he is standing in the doorway.

- Moves faster as the building gets warmer, so try to keep him at a cool sixty degrees.

ANIMATRONICS INVENTORY: BONNIE

- Inhabits Pirate's Cove with Foxy.

- Monitor the figurine on your desk. If the figure is Bonnie, avoid looking at the Pirate's Cove camera, Camera 5. If you do, he'll disable all cameras for some time.

ANIMATRONICS INVENTORY: CHICA

- Stays in the kitchen; you can listen to her by checking Camera 4.
- Keep the music box wound for both her and the Puppet. If you stop hearing the noise from the kitchen, change the music by pressing the button below the Puppet's windup button. If you don't change it, Chica will jump-scare you.

ANIMATRONICS INVENTORY: FOXY

- Like Bonnie, hides in Pirate's Cove.
- If Foxy's figurine appears on your desk, check Camera 5. If you don't check on him, he breaks himself apart and slips pieces into your office. Once he reassembles himself, he'll jump-scare you.

ANIMATRONICS INVENTORY: GODLEN FREDDY

- Appears at random in your office.
- Stare at him for too long and he'll jump-scare you. Instead, put your monitor or tablet up so you're not looking at him, or put on the Freddy mask.

ANIMATRONICS INVENTORY: TOY FREDDY

- Plays "Five Nights With Mr. Hugs" in Parts and Service (Camera 8). In the game, there are three ways into the office and only one door can be closed at a time. Click the cams on Toy Freddy's monitor, then be sure that the appropriate door is closed to prevent Mr. Hugs from getting into Toy Freddy's office.

- If you check on Toy Freddy and see GAME OVER on his screen, that means he's been jump-scared, and now he's coming for you.

ANIMATRONICS INVENTORY: TOY BONNIE

- Sneaks in through a trap door to your right, signaled by a low buzzing sound and flickering lights.

- Put on your Freddy mask and look at him to make him leave.

ANIMATRONICS INVENTORY: TOY CHICA

- Sneaks in through a trap door on the left. She also comes in more often.

- Your only defense is to put on your Freddy mask and look directly at her.

ANIMATRONICS INVENTORY: WITHERED BONNIE

♦ Sneaks in through the same trap door as Toy Bonnie. He will cause audio distortions and disrupt your screen.

♦ Put on the Freddy mask quickly and he'll go away.

ANIMATRONICS INVENTORY: WITHERED CHICA

♦ Enters through the vents and can be blocked using the vent snare.

♦ If she reaches the office, she'll become stuck, preventing you from closing it. Luckily, she also prevents other animatronics (except Mangle) from entering through the vents. Keep in mind that Withered Chica will eventually wiggle free and jump-scare you.

ANIMATRONICS INVENTORY: MANGLE

- Climbs through the vents and can be stopped using the vent snare.

- Once he makes his way to the vent in your office and the vent door opens, she'll hang from the ceiling, cause audio distortions, and jump-scare you.

ANIMATRONICS INVENTORY: THE PUPPET

- Stays in its music box, as usual. Make sure the music box is wound or it'll escape, ending in a jump scare.

ANIMATRONICS INVENTORY: BB AND JJ

- Both animatronics will try to sneak in through the side vent. Make sure to keep it closed until you hear a thud that indicates he or she is gone.

- If BB slips in, he'll disable your flashlight for a short time. If JJ sneaks in, she'll disable the door controls for a short time.

Animatronics Inventory: Springtrap

♦ Climbs through the front vent. He's silent, so all you can do is close the door when you see him.

Animatronics Inventory: Phantom Mangle

♦ Will appear at random on your monitor. If you close your monitor or switch viewing modes, she'll disappear. If left on screen for too long, he'll come into your office and make noise.

Animatronics Inventory: Phantom Freddy

♦ Materializes at random in your office. Shine your flashlight at him quickly to make him disappear, otherwise, he'll jump-scare you, causing you to black out for a short period.

Animatronics Inventory: Phantom BB

♦ Appears at random on your monitor. Close the monitor or switch viewing modes to avoid a jump scare and blackout.

ANIMATRONICS INVENTORY: NIGHTMARE FREDDY + FREDDLES

♦ Freddles will populate your office at random. Shine your flashlight on them to make them disappear. If too many Freddles appear, Nightmare Freddy will jump-scare you!

ANIMATRONICS INVENTORY: NIGHTMARE FREDBEAR AND NIGHTMARE

♦ Appear as a duo. Nightmare Fredbear appears on the left doorway, while Nightmare appears on the right. Only their glowing eyes can be seen, along with a deep laugh sound cue. Shut the doors as soon as you can to stop them from attacking.

ANIMATRONICS INVENTORY: NIGHTMARE BONNIE AND NIGHTMARE MANGLE

♦ Each attacks once per night from the right hall. To fend them off, purchase their plush toys from the Prize Counter on Camera 7 with Faz-Coins (the amount varies based on the difficulty). Once their toy is purchased, they won't attack for the rest of the night.

Animatronics Inventory: Jack O' Chica

♦ As the heat rises in the office, she'll appear in both the right and left doors at the same time. Close the doors before the temperature reaches one hundred degrees to stop her from getting in.

Animatronics Inventory: Nightmarionne

♦ Appears at random in different areas in the office. Avoid leaving your cursor over it or you'll be jump-scared.

Animatronics Inventory: Nightmare Balloon Boy

♦ Sits slumped over in your office throughout the night. Do not shine your light on him if he's sitting down or you'll be jump-scared. If he stands up, shine your light on him to return him to the sitting position or you'll be jump-scared when you turn away.

ANIMATRONICS INVENTORY: CIRCUS BABY

♦ Attacks only once per night, from the right hall. Fend her off by purchasing her plush toy from the Prize Counter on Camera 07.

ANIMATRONICS INVENTORY: BALLORA

♦ Approaches from the left or right hall, disabling your camera feeds. Pay close attention to her music to determine which side she's approaching from, and close the correct door.

ANIMATRONICS INVENTORY: FUNTIME FOXY

♦ Hides behind the curtain in Funtime Cove. The sign outside lists a random "showtime" when Funtime Foxy will come for you. Watch her as the time approaches and until the time passes. This will buy you a few hours until a new time is listed.

ANIMATRONICS INVENTORY: ENNARD

♦ Approaches from the vents and can be tracked only when in motion. Close the vents when you hear a squeaking noise.

ANIMATRONICS INVENTORY: HAPPY FROG, MR. HIPPO, AND PIGPATCH

♦ All use the duct system and hoses to drop into your office. An audio lure will keep Happy Frog away, while the heater or audio lure can be used to deter Mr. Hippo and Pigpatch.

ANIMATRONICS INVENTORY: NEDD BEAR

♦ Also uses the duct system and hoses, but he's only fooled by the audio decoy half of the time. Use heat to deter him from coming into your office through the duct system.

ANIMATRONICS INVENTORY: ORVILLE ELEPHANT

♦ Same as the other Mediocres, but he's only fooled by audio ten percent of the time and is faster than the other Mediocres. Use the heater to repel him!

Animatronics Inventory: Rockstar Freddy

♦ Remains in the office through the night. When he activates, he'll demand a payment of five Faz-Coins. You can turn up the heat to make him malfunction, otherwise he'll jump-scare you.

Animatronics Inventory: Rockstar Bonnie

♦ Appears in your office without his guitar. You must find it quickly on the camera system and double-click it to make him go away.

Animatronics Inventory: Rockstar Chica

♦ Waits outside the left or right doorway of your office. Double-click the WET FLOOR sign to put it in front of the door and make her leave.

Animatronics Inventory: Rockstar Foxy

♦ His parrot will fly across the screen in your office; if you click on it, Rockstar Foxy will appear and either jump-scare you or offer you one of four upgrades: adding 1 percent to your power, resetting the office temperature to sixty degrees, soundproofing the office, or granting you ten Faz-Coins.

ANIMATRONICS INVENTORY: MUSIC MAN

♦ If you make a lot of noise, Music Man will become active, eventually jump-scaring you as he crashes the cymbals in your face. Reducing noise will make him calm down.

ANIMATRONICS INVENTORY: EL CHIP

♦ Periodically interrupts you with advertisements for his restaurant, El Chip's Fiesta Buffet. Click "Skip" or press "Enter" to get rid of them before you attract sound-sensitive animatronics. The higher his difficulty, the more often his ads will appear.

ANIMATRONICS INVENTORY: FUNTIME CHICA

♦ Will occasionally appear and pose accompanied by camera flashes, which will disorient you.

ANIMATRONICS INVENTORY: MOLTEN FREDDY

♦ The fastest of the vent animatronics. You'll hear a laugh when he's about to attack. Close the vent door to send him away.

ANIMATRONICS INVENTORY: SCRAP BABY

♦ Appears by the side of your desk, slumped over, once per night. Next to her is a shock panel, but use it only if you see her move, as it will drain one percent of your power.

ANIMATRONICS INVENTORY: SCRAPTRAP/ WILLIAM AFTON

♦ Attacks only once per night, from the right vent, accompanied by a loud clamoring sound and flickering lights. Close the vent door to keep him out.

ANIMATRONICS INVENTORY: LEFTY

♦ Stays in the closet on Camera 3. If the office becomes too noisy or too hot, he'll jump-scare you. The only way to soothe him is to switch on the Global Music Box. But be careful, as doing so drains your power.

Animatronics Inventory: Phone Guy

♦ Phone Guy simply calls and makes noise. You have only a few seconds to mute his call or listen to his entire message.

Animatronics Inventory: Trash and the Gang

♦ Appear in the office at random and create loud noise while blocking your screen. Mr. Can-Do appears on the camera.

Animatronics Inventory: Old Man Consequences

♦ There's a chance that a subscreen will appear in the top left corner of your screen. Your goal is to press "C" on your keyboard when the fish is on the red dot. If you catch the fish, the screen disappears; otherwise your camera will be inaccessible for some time.

Animatronics Inventory: Helpy

♦ Appears in the top right corner of your office, on the back desk. When you see him, click on him to drive him away. If not, he'll jump-scare you with an air horn.

ANIMATRONICS INVENTORY: DEE DEE

♦ Appears at random and adds new animatronics to your game at difficulty levels one through ten. It won't be clear who has been added; she can either add a character from the start screen or a special character from her own roster . . .

♦ **RWQFSFASXC** makes your office go dark for ten seconds, once per night.

♦ **PLUSHTRAP** appears on Camera 6, sitting in his chair. Scare him away by clicking on him.

♦ **BONNET** will walk across the screen at random. Click her nose or you'll be jump-scared.

- **NIGHTMARE CHICA'S** jaws will close slowly around your field of vision until she jump-scares you. Stop her by using the heater or Power A/C.

- **FOUR MINIREENAS** will cover your screen for one in-game hour.

- **LOLBIT** will cause an audio disturbance. When you hear it, you must quickly type "L-O-L" to make her go away.

ANIMATRONICS INVENTORY: FREDBEAR

- Can be summoned by setting all animatronics to zero and Golden Freddy to one. If Dee Dee summons another animatronic, you'll need to restart the night. Purchase a Death Coin with ten Faz-Coins, then wait for Golden Freddy to show up. When he does, use the Death Coin on him and you'll be jump-scared by Fredbear.

MAPPING THE ANIMATRONICS IN UCN

Springtrap, Withered Chica, Mangle, and Molten Freddy all use the vents

VENTS

Ennard will be visible only when in motion.

Ducts

⚠ = HAPPY FROG

⚠ = MR HIPPO

⚠ = ORVILLE ELEPHANT

⚠ = PIGPATCH

⚠ = NEDD BEAR

ALL ANIMATRONICS CAN COME FROM EITHER DUCT.

Camera 8 – Computer Room: Toy Freddy

Camera 7 – Prize Counter: The Puppet, purchase Death Coins and plushies for Baby, Nightmare Bonnie, and Nightmare Mangle here.

Camera 6 – Funtime Cove: Funtime Foxy

Camera 5 – Pirate's Cove: Bonnie, Foxy

Camera 3 – Supply Closet: Lefty

Camera 4 – Kitchen: Chica

YOU ARE HERE!

Camera 1 – Left Hall: Freddy, Ballora, Rockstar Chica

Camera 2 – Right Hall: Ballora, Nightmare Bonnie, Rockstar Chica, Circus Baby, Nightmare Mangle

On-Camera Feed: Trash and the Gang Phantom Mangle, Phantom BB

Appears in the Office: Golden Freddy, Phantom Freddy, Nightmare Freddy, Nightmarionne, Nightmare BB, Rockstar Freddy, Rockstar Bonnie, Rockstar Foxy, Music Man, Scrap Baby, Helpy, Trash and the Gang

Disruptions: El Chip, Phone Guy, Old Man Consequences, and Funtime Chica will disrupt your play periodically.

Left Door: Nightmare Fredbear, Jack O' Chica

Right Door: Nightmare, Jack O' Chica

Trap Doors:
Left: Toy Chica
Right: Toy Bonnie, Withered Bonnie.

Side Vent: BB, JJ, and Scraptrap all appear at the side vent without warning

Codes, Glitches, and Secrets

MY FRIEND,

IF . . . IF IT

LIFE . . . LIF

BUT THAT

PICNIC W

"WHAT'S

Y'KNOW,

AND FI

PRET

YOU S

Y'KN

SAN

SUC

XOR/Shadow Dee Dee

Sounds to Listen For:

When playing in 50/20 mode, a new animatronic called XOR, or Shadow Dee Dee, will appear, even if Dee Dee Repel is active. She is colorless and eyeless, and arrives accompanied by garbled audio. She eventually calls her entire roster of animatronics, with around seven seconds between the spawn of each. The order goes: RWQFSFASXC, Plushtrap, Nightmare Chica, Bonnet, Minireenas, and Lolbit. She can also very rarely appear in normal play.

Death Lines

Most of the animatronics have "death lines" dialogue they speak after killing you.

♦ Mangle: He's here and always watching. The one you shouldn't have killed.

♦ Nightmare: "I am your wickedness made flesh."

♦ The Puppet: "The others are like animals, but I am very aware."

♦ Withered Chica: "I was the first. I saw everything."

♦ Ballora: "You wanted to let me in."

If you're treated to one Mr. Hippo's extended death lines, settle in! He goes on several lengthy diatribes relating to himself and his friend Orville Elephant. Don't bother trying to skip through it; just sit back, relax, and let Mr. Hippo have his moment.

Old Man Consequences

If all other characters are set to zero and Old Man Consequences is set to one, catching a fish will result in being sent to Old Man Consequences' pond. Old Man Consequences will ask you to "come and sit with me a while," prompting you to press "Enter." When this is done, Old Man Consequences concludes, "Leave the demon to his demons. Rest your own soul. There is nothing else."

Some players have said that by pressing "A" and "D" above the pond, the game will crash. Music can apparently be heard in the background that sounds like robotic screaming.

Lore and Theories

INTERMISSIONS:
TOY CHICA: THE HIGH SCHOOL YEARS

The first unlockable intermission portrays Toy Chica as a high school student who obsesses over various other "boys" at her school, including Freddy, Toy Bonnie, the Puppet, Funtime Foxy, Pigpatch, and the Twisted Wolf from The Twisted Ones. She details in her diary entries how she plans to lure the boys inside and then they'll be hers "forever." Each entry explains, "There is only one thing that could possibly go wrong" before everything resets and Toy Chica has a new target.

In the last cut scene, Toy Chica explains that she's once again brokenhearted, but that tomorrow is another day and that she knows she'll find another guy for her. As she writes in her diary against a tree, her school bag can be seen behind her filled with body parts of the various "guys" (animatronics) she loved.

DOES THAT LOCKER
BEHIND CHICA
SAY "EXOTIC
BUTTERS"?!

INTERMISSIONS: BEAR OF VENGEANCE

This intermission shows various cut scenes portraying Freddy and Foxy as enemies in feudal Japan. Every time Freddy confronts Foxy, he ends up having to perform some sort of household chore for the villain after being defeated in battle. Freddy always vows to seek vengeance the next time.

The title screens are in Japanese, and Freddy and Foxy's lines are spoken in Japanese; however there are English subtitles. Some fans have noted that the English subtitles don't quite match the spoken Japanese.

FINAL INTERMISSION: GOLDEN FREDDY

After unlocking all the cut scenes from both intermissions, you will be shown Golden Freddy sitting in darkness. He twitches violently as he approaches the screen before fading away into the darkness and away from the screen.

Fan Theories

♦ Who are you and where are you? –

Many fans posit that the animatronics' death lines indicate you are playing as William Afton, trapped in Hell. Support for their theory comes from Cassette Man, whom fans believe to be Henry, Afton's old partner, condemning his "old friend" to "burn" at the end of *Pizzeria Simulator*. Some of the animatronics' death lines include the words *burn* and *flame* and *fire*.

♦ Golden Freddy –

Some fans believe that Golden Freddy's final cut scene, where he twitches and retreats into darkness, means that his spirit has not been put to rest and that he is, or will be, seeking revenge.

♦ The One You Should Not Have Killed –

A few different animatronics' death lines use the phrase "the one you should not have killed." Mangle and Withered Chica's death lines suggest this person is a boy, but who exactly is the one you should not have killed? Some fans believe it's Golden Freddy. One of Orville Elephant's death lines says, "He tried to release you, he tried to release us. But I'm not gonna let that happen. I will hold you here, I will keep you here, no matter how many times they burn us." Is the person whom you should not have killed residing in "Hell," haunting and torturing Afton, as some fans suggest?

♦ The Face –

Some players have noted that a child's face appears in the game at random intervals. Could this be "the one you should not have killed"?

♦ TOY CHICA'S HIGH SCHOOL YEARS –
Some fans suggest that the different methods laid out by Toy Chica to lure the boys "inside" may be ways that William Afton lured children to him in order to kill them.

♦ BEAR OF VENGEANCE –
Fans theorize that the Foxy vs. Freddy drama is actually portraying Freddy as Henry and Foxy as William Afton.

♦ MEDIOCRES DEATH LINES –
During the deaths of Happy Frog and her friends, some fans have suggested that a young girl's voice can be heard echoing what the animatronics are saying. Some have even said that the voice resembles that of Scrap Baby from Pizzeria Simulator.

♦ NIGHTMARE FREDBEAR'S DEATH LINE –
One of Nightmare Fredbear's death lines says, "Let me put you back together, then take you apart all over again." Some fans believe that this ties into the iconic Fredbear plushie quote from FNAF 4: "I will put you back together."

Chapter 8

THE BOOKS

Following the overwhelming success of the video game series, *FNAF* creator Scott Cawthon worked to expand the lore and tell a bigger story through the eyes of a teenager affected by the events that took place at Freddy Fazbear's Pizza. *The Silver Eyes*, *The Twisted Ones*, and *The Fourth Closet*, all written by Scott Cawthon and Kira Breed-Wrisley, are novels set in the *FNAF* universe. The story follows Charlie, the daughter of Henry, founder of Fredbear's Family Diner and the engineer behind the original animatronics.

Debates have been raging among the fans about how the books tie into the games, but, for now, their connection remains shrouded in mystery. While the novels share many of the same elements as the games, they have some clear differences. The setting of the pizzeria feels the same, but the new story involves a cast of characters that interact directly with the animatronics . . . and animatronics that interact with one another.

THE SILVER EYES

Ten years after the horrific murders at Freddy Fazbear's Pizza, the people of Hurricane, Utah, have mostly moved on. But Charlie and her childhood friends, who were directly affected by those events, can never forget. The old gang is thrown together again for a memorial service marking the anniversary of the children who were murdered—including their friend, Michael Brooks.

To face their tragic past, the group decides to visit the old pizza place one last time . . . When they arrive at the long-abandoned location, however, they're surprised to discover that the restaurant and its animatronics are very much intact. Little has changed for Freddy and his friends, and many of its nightmares have remained.

THE TWISTED ONES

The second book in the series takes place one year later and opens on Charlie, who is now in her freshman year of college in the neighboring town of New Harmony. Studying robotics like her father before her, Charlie has found herself connected to her past than ever. After a tornado tears through Hurricane, a body is discovered, and it bears injuries that resemble those from a spring lock suit. Police chief Clay Burke reaches out to Charlie for help in solving the murders, but on their hunt for the killer, they unearth more sinister monsters long forgotten. And these monsters won't stop until they have what they want: Charlie.

Five Nights at Freddy's

THE TWISTED ONES

DON'T TRUST YOUR EYES

THE FOURTH CLOSET

The third book picks up a few months from where *The Twisted Ones* left off, and John can't seem to shake the feeling that something is wrong with Charlie. Too bad John seems to be the only one actually interested in investigating the mysterious circumstances of Charlie's supposed death and miraculous reappearance. While the whole gang wants to forget about Freddy's, a new animatronic pizzeria opens in town. With it comes a string of new kidnappings and new nightmares. John, Jessica, Marla, and Carlton join forces to figure out what's going on and try to stop more children from going missing. But the real mystery is what happened to Charlie . . . and the legacy her father's creations left behind.

November 1, 1982

TODDLER SNATCHED

CHARLIE APPEARS TO HAVE A TWIN, SAMMY, WHO DISAPPEARED, BUT LITTLE IS KNOWN ABOUT HIM.

CHARACTER PROFILE: CHARLIE

Charlie grew up in Hurricane, but left ten years earlier to live with her Aunt Jen, who taught her to be fiercely independent and self-sufficient. Throughout the course of the series, Charlie becomes increasingly determined to find answers to the mysteries of her haunted past, clinging to the few childhood memories that have stuck with her. Though Charlie finds it hard to open up to others, she very much values her friends and the special bond they share.

CHARACTER PROFILE: JOHN

Charlie's childhood friend and crush, John is a writer and a keen observer of the world around him. He cares deeply for Charlie, always offering her support no matter how difficult or dangerous the situation. John is wise for his age, and he can often be quite sarcastic.

CHARACTER PROFILE: JESSICA

After the murders ten years earlier, Jessica moved to New York with her family. She grew up to be sophisticated and pretty, with a love of fashion only surpassed by her love of forensics. While people often underestimate her, Jessica frequently finds herself taking on the role of leader and strategist. She is one of Charlie's best friends.

CHARACTER PROFILE: AUNT JEN

Jen stepped in as Charlie's guardian after the death of her father, Henry. She taught Charlie to be ready for the harshness of the world, which is the reason why Charlie is so independent. Aunt Jen believes painful memories are better left forgotten.

> "*Live in the present moment*, her Aunt Jen said often, and Charlie had taken it to heart. *Don't dwell on the past; don't worry about things that may never happen.*"
> —from *The Silver Eyes*

CHARACTER PROFILE: CLAY BURKE

Clay Burke is the chief of police in Hurricane, Utah, as well as the father of Charlie's childhood friend Carlton. Clay is one of the few main characters who knows the more intimate details of the case of the missing children. At first, he doesn't buy into the supernatural rumors surrounding Freddy Fazbear's Pizza, but by the time *The Twisted Ones* takes place, he's one of Charlie's fiercest allies and valued for his astute observations and sleuthing skills.

> "'You know, I wasn't the chief back then. I was still a detective, and I was working on those disappearances. To this day, it was the worst thing I've ever had to see. It's not something to joke about.'"
> —from *The Silver Eyes*

CHARACTER PROFILE: WILLIAM AFTON

Business partner to Charlie's late father, William Afton was also one of the prime suspects in the missing children case from ten years ago. Though he was never officially charged, William left town quickly and his current whereabouts are unknown.

"Before him stood someone who had spent so much of his life fighting like a cornered rat that he had taken on the mantle of bitter sadism as an integral part of himself. He would strike out against others and revel in their pain, feeling righteously that the world owed him his cruel pleasures."
—from *The Silver Eyes*

CHARACTER PROFILE: HENRY

Charlie's father, the founder of Fredbear's Family Diner, was an engineer with a childlike sense of imagination. He personally built all the animatronics at the restaurant. Charlie remembers him as a good man, but—unbeknownst to her—he took many dark secrets to his grave.

"'*We* were the secret life. His real life was his work; it was what mattered. We were his guilty pleasure, the thing he got to love and sneak away to have time with, something he kept hidden away from the dangers of what he did in his *real* world. And when he was with us, there was always a part of him that was back in reality, whatever that was for him.'" —from *The Silver Eyes*

ANIMATRONICS INVENTORY: THEODORE

This purple rabbit was the first of Charlie's father's gifts and the simplest of his creations. It could wave its hand, tilt its head, and repeat a recording of Henry saying, "I love you, Charlie." Theodore was made to give three-year-old Charlie a friend in her dark, lonely house. After deteriorating for years in Charlie's abandoned home, Theodore can no longer wave, and most of her father's recording has degraded.

ANIMATRONICS INVENTORY: STANLEY

Bobbing his head like a racehorse, this white unicorn gallops on a track around Charlie's room at the touch of a button. Though he can still move, Stanley has rusted considerably after years of disuse.

ANIMATRONICS INVENTORY: ELLA

Ella was built to match Charlie's size as a small child. When the wheel at the foot of Charlie's bed is turned, Ella exits her mini-closet, holding up a cup for a tea party. Since Ella spent her years of neglect inside her closet, she is the most intact of the animatronics, with her fancy dress almost as crisp as the day Charlie left Hurricane.

217

CHARACTER PROFILE: CARLTON

Carlton is a goofy and fun-loving teenage boy who likes to create stories and comedy routines. Conveniently, this all helps to hide how much the troubling events of his childhood affected him.

> "Carlton looked like an older version of his red-headed childhood self. He still had a bit of a baby face, but his features had refined, and his hair was carefully tousled and held in place by some alchemical hair product. He was almost pretty, for a boy, and he wore a black workout shirt, though she doubted he'd ever worked out a day in his life." —from *The Silver Eyes*

CHARACTER PROFILE: MARLA

Marla is determined and strong-willed, with a big personality that can lighten the mood of those around her. She is extremely loyal to those she loves, and is one of the few friends that made sure to stay in touch with Charlie after everyone moved away.

> "She was resolutely positive and assumed that everyone liked her unless they made it clear otherwise, using the proper expletives." —from *The Silver Eyes*

CHARACTER PROFILE: JASON

Marla's younger half-brother. The two often bicker, but they care deeply for each other. As the only young boy in a group of teenagers, Jason often fights to be taken seriously.

> "'Jason, stop it,' Marla said. 'Play with your action figures.' 'I'm not a little kid,' he said. 'Anyway, they're in the car.'" —from *The Silver Eyes*

CHARACTER PROFILE: LAMAR

Smart and hardworking, Lamar is the voice of reason among his friends. His parents have a "five-year plan" in place to guide him to success, like receiving early admission to Cornell. While he may follow his parents' plans dutifully, he won't pass up an opportunity to have fun.

"'I'd forgotten this was a real place.' Lamar smiled, for the first time resembling the little boy Charlie had once known. Charlie smiled back. There was something surreal about the place; she had certainly never told any of her school friends about it." —from *The Silver Eyes*

THE MISSING CHILDREN

Ten years prior to the events of the novel, five children from Hurricane went missing, including Charlie's childhood friend Michael. Their disappearance is tied to Freddy Fazbear's Pizza, but their bodies have never been found, nor has their kidnapper been caught.

"'I want to say,' Joan continued, 'something about the families who are not here. As we all know, Michael was not the only child lost during those terrible few months.' She read out four more names, two girls and two boys. Charlie glanced at Marla. They all knew there had been other children, but Michael's death had loomed so great in all their lives that they had never even talked about the other victims. Now Charlie felt a pang of guilt. To someone, those little girls and boys had been as vital as Michael. To someone, their losses had meant the end of the world. She closed her eyes for a moment. *I can't mourn everyone*, she thought. *No one can.*"
—from *The Silver Eyes*

ANIMATRONICS INVENTORY: TWISTED FREDDY

The once-beloved mascot of Freddy Fazbear's Pizza is a far cry from this eerie, twisted animatronic that seems designed for a much more sinister purpose.

ANIMATRONICS INVENTORY: TWISTED FOXY

"Like the face, the body was smoother than the animatronics that Charlie was used to. It had no fur, and no tail or other animal appendages. It was too large for a human being to wear, probably eight feet tall when standing. Still, Charlie couldn't shake the feeling that she recognized this creature. *Foxy.*

"There was something sick about the creature, a weirdness that gripped her at the most basic, primal level and cried, *This is wrong.*"
—from *The Twisted Ones*

ANIMATRONICS INVENTORY: TWISTED BONNIE

As a child, Jessica was partial to Bonnie due to his "understanding look," and she often confided in him her childhood troubles. But the Bonnie that appears in *The Twisted Ones* is far from understanding.

ANIMATRONICS INVENTORY: TWISTED WOLF

"A wolf's mane ran over the top of its head and down its back. It was stooped over, one arm twisted downward while the other flailed up. Perhaps its control over its limbs was uncertain . . . Yet while the eyes held a steady light, the rest of the creature was in flux . . . One moment it was a groomed and agile figure covered in silver hair, the next a tattered metal framework, partly coated in rubbery translucent skin."
—from *The Twisted Ones*

ANIMATRONICS INVENTORY: CIRCUS BABY

This sleeker, humanoid animatronic serves William Afton, who calls her "Elizabeth." The true origins of this animatronic are shrouded in mystery, but today she serves only the interests of her twisted "father," and her own bloody, vengeful interests.

FNAF LORE:
CONNECTIONS BETWEEN THE BOOKS AND GAMES

While the books are set in a separate universe from the games, some larger similarities have gotten fans' wheels turning . . .

♦ The Victims: While many fans have been quick to point out that Henry, William Afton, Charlie (Charlotte), and Elizabeth are all characters from the games and books, fans have also noted that two of the original victims in the books (Susie, Fritz) match the names etched on the tombstones in *Pizzeria Simulator*.

♦ Five Becoming One: We don't want to spoil anything for readers, but suffice it to say that Candy Cadet's secret stories in *Pizzeria Simulator* might strike a chord with those who finish reading *The Fourth Closet*.

♦ The Creators: The books offer a closer peek at Henry and William Afton, how their partnership flourished early on, and how their view of the animatronics evolved over time. Thoughtful fans might want to give these sections a closer look to determine how they impact the story of the games as well.

Five Nights at Freddy's: Survival Logbook

Released shortly after *Freddy Fazbear's Pizzeria Simulator*, the *Five Nights at Freddy's: Survival Logbook* offered a chance for *FNAF* fans to put themselves in the shoes of a new night guard at Freddy Fazbear's Pizza and reflect on their first week on the job. The book is divided into five sections, representing a guard's first five nights on the job, and is filled with interactive quizzes, activities, and "incident reports" to fill out. There are also a few secrets hiding in those pages that can help solve the many mysteries in *Freddy Fazbear's Pizzeria Simulator*!

FREDDY FAZBEAR'S PIZZA

SURVIVAL

SECURITY LOGBOOK

Everything employees need to survive
a first five nights on the job!

WHAT'S NEXT FOR *FNAF*?

There are new short stories forthcoming, and there are sure to be more games. The only thing we can say for certain is that whatever's next for Five Nights at Freddy's is certain to fill your nightmares . . . Sweet dreams.